Ketchum's Folly

Ketchum's Folly

by Jay Underwood

LANCELOT PRESS
Hantsport, N.S.

ISBN 0-88999-553-2
Published 1995

ALL RIGHTS RESERVED. No part of this book may be reproduced in any form without written permission of the publisher except brief quotations embodied in critical articles or reviews.

LANCELOT PRESS LIMITED, Hantsport, Nova Scotia.
Office and production facilities situated on Highway No. 1, 1/2 mile east of Hantsport.

MAILING ADDRESS:
P.O. Box 425, Hantsport, N.S. B0P 1P0

PHONE:
(902) 684-9129

ACKNOWLEDGEMENT: This book has been published with the assistance of the Canada Council and the Nova Scotia Department of Education, Cultural Affairs Division.

For my sons, Andrew and Derek,
with the hope they will never be afraid to dream,
or be too afraid to make a dream come true.

Acknowledgements

I am indebted to a great number of people for their assistance in gathering information for this book, but in particular to my father, Peter Underwood, and Douglas MacKay, editor-in-chief of the Halifax *Daily News* for their help in making me, if only slightly, computer literate.

I must also thank the staff of the Public Archives of Nova Scotia; Audrey Johnston of the New Brunswick Archives, Fredericton; the National Archives, Ottawa; Jane Fullerton, Janet Bishop and Andrea Kirkpatrick of the New Brunswick Museum, Saint John; staff of the Nova Scotia Museum; Maritime Museum of the Atlantic; Queens' University library special collections department; the Guided Ground Transportation Institute, Kingston, Ont.; the staff of the Colchester-East Hants Regional Library; Steve Ridlington, officer in charge at Fort Beausejour National Historic Site; Carol Arrowsmith of the Institution of Civil Engineers; Andrea Owens of the University of Liverpool; Frank Myrskog of *The Daily News* graphic arts department, and all those people who offered their versions of the tales told of the Chignecto Ship Railway, including my wife's late grandfather, Bedford Palmer.

Special thanks to Tom McCoag of Amherst, who patiently photographed the material held at Fort

Beausejour NHS, and to Nicholas Johnson of The Stock Press, Baldwin N.Y. for tracking down a copy of the bonds sold in London to finance Ketchum's grand scheme.

The keen reader will notice that none of the measurements in this history are given in metric equivalents. This is simply because it was not the parlance of Henry Ketchum, and conversion is often bothersome and leaves more room for error.

Finally I must thank my wife, Kathy, who may not always completely understand my fascination with long-dead and unsuccessful railway ventures, but tolerates it nevertheless.

Contents

Acknowledgements 6
Introduction 9

One
I Should Not Have Come Here 13

Two
In Good Company 22

Three
The Company Will Satisfy the Government 35

Four
The Company Was Misled 42

Five
A Baby In Its Mother's Arms 53

Six
A Hopeless Task 61

Seven
One of the Most Astounding Frauds 73

Eight
I Thought This Chignecto Business Was Dead 82

Appendix 102
Epilogue 126
Bibliography 128

Introduction

What is it a truly original genius will not improve? Everything is prolific of novelty in the hand of a master. His ideas are not the crude conceptions of dullness; nor his sentiments either the vapid yawning of a listless, or the insignificant prattle of an empty heart. He generally plans entirely for himself, and always executes in a manner preceded by nothing similar. The light he strikes out is so singular, and withal so true, that we are equally pleased with what we never saw before, and surprised that we now only see it for the first time.

John Moir,
Gleanings, 1785

Even today, after man has been to the moon and regularly takes jaunts into space, the idea of a huge ship being transported by rail over dry land in order to avoid stormy waters elsewhere sounds like science fiction. Perhaps that was the Chignecto Ship Railway's problem.

It seems to me a tragedy that no monument exists to celebrate Henry Ketchum's attempt at what many considered to be as impossible as space travel, other than the mounds of long grassed-over earth and tide-worn ruins of a dock at a provincial park in Tidnish, Nova Scotia. All traces of the Chignecto Ship Railway's history have been left scattered about, much like the track that was torn up and relaid elsewhere, or the stonework of the great lift houses, that now forms the breakwater at the ferry terminal at Cape Tormentine, New Brunswick.

Despite all that has been written, and rewritten, about the railway, there appears to be no single body of work which considers all the facts and fantasies that have become entangled in the folklore of the Maritimes.

I must confess, I tend to be a bit of a romantic when it comes to the Chignecto Ship Railway. How else can I explain the urge to recreate Ketchum's concept in miniature, the working scale model which I so proudly display at every opportunity? The romance grew in spite of knowing what such an attitude has done to the reality of history.

It is not my intention here to use the failure of the ship railway as a means to protest what is so often seen as an anti-Maritime Canada attitude in Ottawa. The reality is that no such sentiment ever existed toward Ketchum or his scheme. There was no other motive to build the model than the sheer joy of being able to watch it work, close one's eyes and imagine the grandeur of a ship riding majestically over dry land, as if it were cruising a mill pond.

This book, on the other hand, is an attempt to put the Chignecto Ship Railway story into proper perspective. It offers a more comprehensive, but by no means definitive account of its history, as gathered from the myriad footnotes and essays previously published, and uses material from Ketchum's own documents never before made public. In doing this it is my hope that the railway will be elevated from being nothing more than an oddity, to being a living, breathing piece of Maritimes history.

Engineers and journalist are alike in one way. They seek to build monuments to themselves — engineers by their works, journalists by their words. Sir Benjamin Baker's monument is the Forth Bridge, Eiffel has his tower. Ketchum never got such a monument, unless one considers his railway to be a folly — one of those elaborate but unnecessary buildings British gentry used to erect on their estates for no particular reason.

What is truly unfortunate, is that Ketchum is remembered for his failure and not his spectacular successes on railways elsewhere, especially in New Brunswick.

Hopefully Ketchum, the engineer, and I as a journalist, can share this book as a monument to the dream he attempted to realize, and which I keep alive in miniature.

Elmsdale,
March, 1993

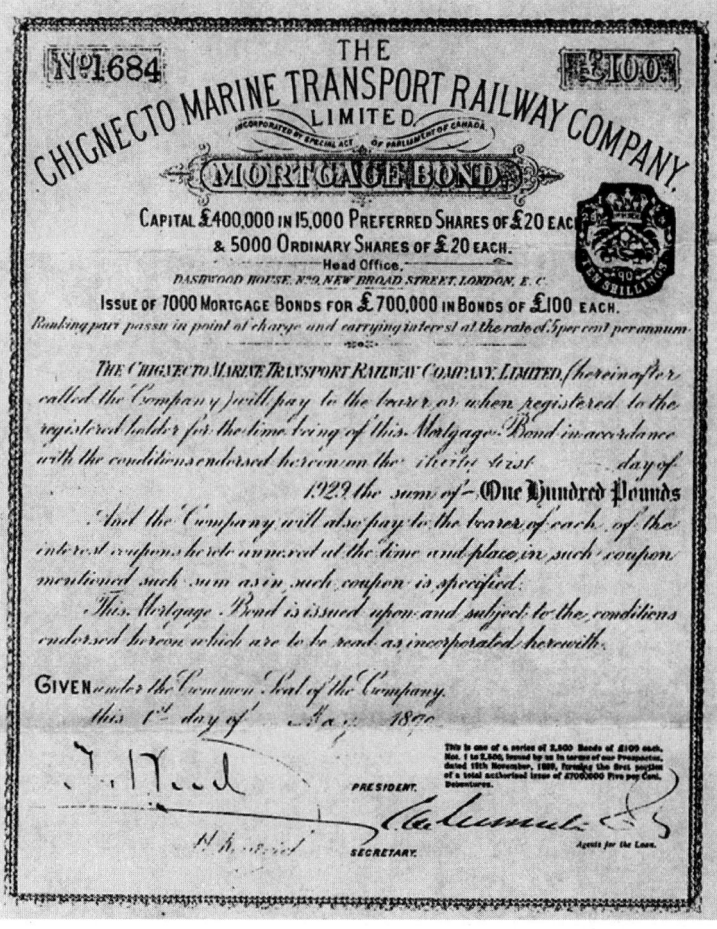

One

I Should Not Have Come Here

When the 270-foot dredge *Charles R. Huntley* limped into Halifax Harbour on Nov. 17 1990, the 12 crew members of the then 64-year-old vessel were well aware they had narrowly avoided paying the heavy toll often taken by the Atlantic Ocean. On its way to a job in the Bay of Fundy from the Gulf of St. Lawrence, the *Huntley* ran into rough weather 40 miles off Halifax, and began taking on water. A helicopter and Coast Guard vessels were dispatched to lift off injured crew and tow the *Huntley* safely into port. Other ships have been less fortunate.

If the Atlantic's often unpredictable and unmerciful weather were not trial enough, the passage of ships between the Gulf and the New England coast necessarily takes them close to Sable Island, the graveyard of the Atlantic. Around that shifting sandy bar, barely five miles long, lies the wreckage of countless vessels, wooden and steel, which the sea has claimed for its own — a tribute demanded from the mere mortals who dare to trespass on those waters.

Owners of today's bigger ships can afford to scoff at the threat posed by a voyage such as that of the *Charles R. Huntley*, but merchants and mariners of little more than 200 years ago enjoyed no such luxury. Every trip was fraught with danger, and undertaken with the understanding of the potential for disaster. Until the construction of railway links between New England's ports and Canada's commercial capitals in Toronto, Montreal and Quebec, the sea route from the St. Lawrence, through the Canso Straits and out into the open Atlantic was a necessary evil. The inventive minds of many men were brought to bear on this problem, and the search for a safer route took on as much importance for the commercial interests of the region as had the European search for the Northwest Passage.

The first solution proposed by the Abbe de la Loutre, during the French regime, was a canal to connect the Gulf of St. Lawrence with the Bay of Fundy. In 1783 Colonel Robert Morris of the Royal Engineers championed the idea from a purely military and naval point of view. It was not until 1822, when the government of New Brunswick instructed provincial land surveyor Robert C. Minnette to make the first survey for a canal, that governments got involved in any official capacity. Three years later, in 1825, New Brunswick's Governor, Sir Howard Douglas engaged the services of engineer Francis Hall to report on the proposed construction of a canal along the lines of the Minette survey.

Sir Thomas Telford, one of the leading British engineers of the time supported Hall's findings, which were later bolstered by an 1843 study conducted by Captain H.O. Crowley of the Royal Engineers. Crowley had been commissioned jointly by the governments of Canada, New Brunswick and Prince Edward Island.

In the meantime, with railway technology developing so rapidly, the public's attention naturally turned in that direction, and it was not long before it was proposed to use steamship lines established on either side of the isthmus to transship freight over a railway between the Peticodiac River on the Bay of Fundy, and Shediac, on the Gulf of St. Lawrence. In 1853 a company was formed to build the 18-mile line — from Moncton to Pointe du Chene, a project that had to be completed by the Government of New

Brunswick in 1858. It seemed to be a successful alternative to a canal: cargo from the gulf ports was off-loaded at Pointe du Chene, taken across the isthmus and reloaded onto steamers on the Bay of Fundy. By 1860 the line had been extended to Saint John, while further east, a 55-mile line from Pictou to Truro was built by the Government of Nova Scotia. Shortly thereafter, as the railway boom continued in the region, a railway from Sackville to Cape Tormentine, and branches of the Intercolonial Railway to Buctouche, Richibucto, Chatham, Caraquet and Dalhousie were opened, all a reflection of the volume of trade between the Gulf and Saint John and the United States.

The solution was a short-lived success, however. It was not appropriate for bulk cargo such as lumber, coal, gypsum, plaster, building stone, potatoes, deals and fish. These were difficult and expensive items to load and unload, so little saving was achieved by using the overland route.

The focus then turned to trade that might be established between the western lake ports and New England if vessels could sail the whole route without breaking cargo. A canal would save vessels, now passing from the St. Lawrence to Saint John via the Canso Straits, some 500 miles, and would shorten the distance for vessels bound for Portland, Boston and other Atlantic ports by as much as 300 miles.

Shipping industry officials were convinced this new route would save ships going from Shediac, Charlottetown or Baie Verte to Saint John at least nine or ten days and vessels bound for Europe from Saint John could shorten their voyages by nearly two weeks. Another benefit of this "inland route" would be the smaller insurance premiums (considerably higher for vessels sailing the Atlantic coast of Nova Scotia than for those sailing the Bay of Fundy) that were anticipated.

In 1869 the Nova Scotia Legislature approved the incorporation of a company to build a "inland route" canal as a private venture. The province's chief engineer of public works, John Page, was ordered to study all the previous surveys for a canal across the Isthmus of Chignecto, and additional surveys were ordered by the Dominion government. In 1871 a thorough survey of the isthmus was carried out by F. Baillarge, assistant chief engineer of public works. In the following year, Sir Cazimir Gzowski and Samuel Keefer surveyed and recommended a canal approximately on what would become the route of Henry Ketchum's ship railway. The estimated cost of this canal was $7,100,000.

A royal commission headed by Sir Hugh Allan (founder of the Allan shipping line and later of the Canadian Pacific Railway) and businessmen from other provinces was appointed in 1871 to investigate Canada's entire canal system. The commission recommended the Chignecto Canal be given top priority, and the Conservative government of Prime Minister Sir John A. Macdonald approved the construction. Macdonald budgeted $1,000,000 for the project, but in 1875, Alexander Mackenzie's Liberals, struck another commission which reflected Liberal suspicion of Tory projects by reporting unfavorably on the Chignecto canal. It was later alleged that the second commission was appointed for the sole purpose of defeating the project, and indeed, the Mackenzie regime had dedicated itself to cost cutting worthy of the 1990's. For a time public and political interest in the canal subsided, only to be revived when Henry Ketchum proposed his bold plan.

The problems of Atlantic storms, canals and the wretched perils of maritime commerce would have had little impact on the early years of Henry George Cloppers Ketchum. Born Feb. 26 1839 at Fredericton, Ketchum's formative years were spent in the struggle for survival.

He was born into that remarkable breed known as the New Brunswick Loyalist, determined Anglican stock who drew strength in equal measure from their faith in God and confidence in their own abilities. His paternal grandfather, a former New England militia colonel, was something of a hero around Woodstock, N.B. for having tobogganed across frozen land in the dead of one particularly dreadful winter, in order to deliver food to a stranded village of starving residents.

As W.C. Milner noted in his unpublished biography of Ketchum, "his father died suddenly when he was little more than an infant. His mother was left in straightened circumstances, but being a high-spirited woman, she went to work to keep her family, without inviting outside aid. Her son as he grew up picked up his education by bits and scraps as best he could partly at the Grammar School and partly at university. He was able to get, at the University of New Brunswick, the first diploma issued for civil engineering." In this respect, Ketchum had already become a pioneer in his field, with accomplishments that would be respected at least by other engineers in the years to follow, if not by the public at large.

His obituary, as recorded in the minutes of the proceedings of the Institution of Civil Engineers, notes Ketchum entered King's College University early in 1854, to study engineering under Thomas McMahon Creagan. Ketchum proved to be so adept at the engineer's craft that he was frequently excused from classes to obtain experience working on the Moncton-Pointe du Chene line. The line which became Ketchum's classroom had opened with great ceremony in Saint John, Sept. 14 1853 (Ketchum would have been 14 at the time) with a two-mile parade which included teams of horses pulling models of a fully-rigged clipper and a steamship.

When Ketchum graduated in 1862, engineer/historian Bruce Higgins notes: "He was truly a pioneer of the 'co-operative program' of engineering education in the Atlantic region." A great deal of this on-the-job education stood Ketchum in good stead. According to Milner,

> He worked in the Crown Land Office, where he obtained a certificate as a deputy land surveyor. He drafted the plans for the first bridge built across the Tantramar River. Unable to obtain employment, he learned telegraphy and was employed as an operator

at Fredericton. In 1856, he was employed by Mr. A.L. Light, chief engineer, in the drafting department of the E&NA Ry. (European and North American Railway) then commenced between Saint John and Shediac. His work was always satisfactory to his superiors and led to his promotion to the position of assistant engineer. He laid out and located a piece of railway near Sussex Vale, 17 miles long without a curve, which can be seen today, regarded at the time as a fine piece of engineering.

The association with Mr. Light was to launch the international journey that would give birth to Ketchum's ship railway, a journey that would first take him to Brazil. Light was among the foreign, mostly British, engineers hired to build the Sao Paulo Railway, and he took young Ketchum with him as an assistant engineer in August of 1860. If the Sussex Vale line was the first testimonial to Ketchum's ability, the Sao Paulo, again unrecognized by his countrymen, was the second.

The railway, one of the most circuitous in the world, also has one of the steepest profiles. It connected Sao Paulo, located high on an inland plateau, with the coffee port of Santos on the mosquito-infested coast. Between the two towns lay dense jungle, wild animals, swamps breeding typhoid and yellow fever for the unprotected, and an elevation of more than "half a mile high," according to Ketchum's own description.

At 21 years of age, Ketchum's responsibilities on the line were onerous, and included the design and construction of the Mogy viaduct, a twelve-span bridge, "180 feet high, constructed of iron columns on granite piers." His determination to get a job done quickly, and done well, was evident in Brazil; the Mogy viaduct was built within seven months.

The time Ketchum spent in Brazil was, by his own accounts, among the most miserable in his life. He wrote to his solicitor, Fredericton lawyer George Diblee, Nov. 8 1860, from the contractor's office in Santos, "I am getting on very well here considering the circumstances, but the climate is not nearly as good as I was led to believe." He went on to complain about the "witherable heat of a Brazilian summer," and of his own recent ill-health. " I suffered two attacks of sickness (recently)" he wrote, "but they did not last long."

His workers did not fare as well: "I sent a man to the hospital from my district with the yellow fever day before yesterday ... the climate is very nasty and rainy," he told Diblee, but, "I have a good salary and a better position than I expected, and therefore should be contented but I must say that if I had known beforehand what this country was, I should not have come here."

The climate and disease were not all that troubled young Ketchum. In the same letter he described his all too-close encounter with an alligator in the surrounding swamps: "The brute was within five yards of me — my servant man was so frightened that he almost upset the canoe. It would not have been very pleasant to come in contact with his jaws."

Earlier that week, he told Diblee, a jaguar had entered the camp and attempted to carry a man off into the jungle. Ketchum also told Diblee he had seen "all manner of snakes, including a two-headed serpent." If the life was miserable, the rewards at least proved to be substantial. Milner notes that,

> ... when that railway was completed, he went to England. The contractors, Sir James Fox & Sons, were so pleased with his services that the morning after his arrival at the hotel in London, he found on his breakfast table a note from them enclosing a cheque for 500 pounds.

Going to London was a natural pilgrimage for a young engineer eager to learn more, and ready to sample a less physically demanding climate than that of Brazil. The city was the intellectual center of the greatest engineering minds in the world, men who had built great bridges, tunnels and ships and designed some of the finest railways in the world.

It was a place where a young engineer could test his mental mettle against the giants of the profession at the Institution of Civil Engineers. Founded Jan. 2 1818, by Telford, and incorporated under a royal charter June 3 1828, the institution was dedicated to the "advancement of mechanical science, and the training of civil engineers in that species of knowledge which is essential to them." The building on Great George Street in Westminster housed a library of more than 5,000 books, and there can be no doubt that it was while in London that Ketchum would learn about ship railway technology, and its practical application to a problem back home.

The plan he would devise was a model of understated simplicity, couched in the matter-of-fact phraseology of the profession:

> The line of the ship railway is 17 miles long in a straight line from Fort Lawrence on the Bay of Fundy to Tidnish on the gulf side, and is practically without a gradient. There are to be 2 tracks, with rails of 100 pounds each to the yard ... the Fort Lawrence Dock is a spacious basin, capable of containing at a time 6 ships of 1,000 tons each. It is excavated 40 feet deep, is 500 feet long and 300 feet wide. Walls of massive masonry rise on either side of the gate, to retain the waters of the basin. A gate 30 feet high and 60 feet wide opens at high water to admit shipping. When admitted, the vessel is floated over a gridiron (which forms a movable part of the track), which, with the cradle upon it, is immersed to the bottom of the lifting dock to receive the vessel for transportation. There is no danger whatever of injury to vessels from being strained, either from being raised up vertically from the dock, or during transportation, or depositing again in the water by the means proposed to be used in this railway, which will be a great improvement on other lifting docks and marine railways. Keel blocks in the center of

the cradle and adjustable bilge blocks afford ample support to the sides and bottom of the vessel, and the cradle rests on springs affording just sufficient elasticity to render any strain impossible without causing oscillation. The cradle is about 230 feet long, 40 feet wide; it is carried on 192 wheels, and consists of three sections.

The hydraulic rams and presses to lift vessels to the level of the track are 20 in number, 10 on each side of the track. The length of their stroke is 40 feet. Each set of lifting apparatus is composed of 2 cylinders, the inner one performing the functions of a piston and ram, and the outer one, which is called the press. When the vessel is floated over the cradle and received in place, the whole mass (comprising ship, gridiron and cradle) is raised to the level of the main track. The gridiron is then locked to the sides of the quay, this forming a bridged platform. Hydraulic machinery will then be applied to haul the cradle and vessel from the gridiron to the track of the railway. A couple of locomotives are attached, and the journey across the isthmus can then be proceeded with. To sustain such great weights, the roadbed is of the most solid construction and the foundation of the most stable character. Arriving at Tidnish, the vessel is placed over the gridiron in the lifting dock by hydraulic capstans and lowered into the dock.

Two

In Good Company

With his reputation made for him in Brazil, Ketchum was quickly accepted by his colleagues in London. According to Milner,

> This work gave Mr. Ketchum a certain standing with the leading engineers of the day — Sir James Brunlees, Sir Benjamin Baker and others, whose confidence and friendship he retained during life. Mr. Ketchum became an associate of the Institute of Civil Engineers (British) in 1866 and a full member in 1878.

This "standing" gave Ketchum access to the great works of all the institute's members, key among them Sir Benjamin Baker, whose presence on the board of directors of the Chignecto Marine Transport Railway Co. would add prestige to Ketchum's plan when it came time to raise capital from British investors.

Baker was an engineer of considerable acclaim. A year younger than Ketchum, he had become an assistant to Sir John Fowler in 1862. By 1867 Baker had written a series of articles on long span bridges, and was acknowledged as an expert in cantilever design. The Forth Bridge was built between 1883 and 1890, winning Fowler a baronetcy and

Baker, who became a full partner in 1875, a knighthood.

The Forth bridge fell into the hands of Baker and Fowler by a stroke of luck and a freak of nature. The original engineer was to have been Sir Thomas Bouch, who had designed the bridge over the Firth of Tay, opened in 1878. When a windstorm blew down the girders in the middle of the Tay bridge in 1879, taking the Dundee mail train with it, Bouch's contract to build the Forth bridge was cancelled, and handed to Baker and Fowler, with Sir William Arrol as contractor.

Baker's accomplishments were not limited to bridges. In 1869 he was responsible, with Fowler, for construction of the London Underground Railway. He engineered the transportation of Cleopatra's Needle from Egypt to its site today on the Thames Embankment in London, and took part in the design of the first of the Aswan dams. In the U.S., he was consulted by James B. Eads, the eminent American engineer of the day (and a man who may have unwittingly had a role in the failure of Ketchum's scheme) then engaged in the construction of the St. Louis bridge over the Mississippi. Baker went on to become president of the Institute of Civil Engineers from 1895-96, and a member of the prestigious Royal Society.

Throughout his involvement with Ketchum, Baker never doubted the feasibility of a ship railway across the Isthmus of Chignecto, and his endorsement should put to rest the notion that Ketchum's railway was a hare-brained scheme that never would have worked.

"A ship railway," Sir Benjamin asserted, "is the logical result of the continual improvement in railway methods from the time of the first railway to the present. If it is possible to raise vessels and transport them overland with safety and economy, why should they be compelled to make great detours costing time and money?"

There was more than Baker's professional support to bolster Ketchum's concept; the principal of a ship railway was not entirely new. Lifting docks in Malta, Bombay, London and San Francisco had been used successfully to lift loaded vessels out of the water for repairs. Dry dock companies in many parts of the world were accustomed to moving vessels by rail for various distances. There was one instance reported from Florida in 1886 of a steamer being hauled by rail some fifty miles without damage. Indeed, a ship railway had been proposed years before as an alternative to construction of the Suez Canal, by another of Ketchum's acquaintances, Sir James Brunlees.

Brunlees' plan was made redundant when construction of a canal was begun in 1856. The 100-mile long waterway was calculated to take weeks off the voyage from Europe to Asia, allowing ships to avoid the often treacherous trip around the southern tip of Africa, the Cape of Good Hope. Instead there was a 16-18 hour cruise through the canal.

Brunlees had envisaged his railway to run in a direct line from one side of the Sinai divide to the other, multiple track all the way, with little or no grade, a plan copied almost exactly by Ketchum thirty years later, and for which Ketchum was quick to give credit in his May 15 1881 letter to the federal government:

> I am indeed indebted to Sir James Brunlees Esq., vice-president of the Institution of Civil Engineers, for a description of a ship railway across the Isthmus of Suez, proposed by him and the late Mr. E.B. Webb C.E. to the late Emperor of the French in 1859, in place of the Suez canal now in operation.
>
> Their scheme was to transport ships of the largest tonnage then in existence by means of locomotives of special construction at a speed of twenty miles an hour. The ships were to rest on cradles supported by numerous wheels and springs, resting on a railway composed of five pairs of rail and level throughout its entire length. They reported that "a ship would be able to make better use of her sails on a railway than on a canal;" that the system would offer all the facilities that are provided by graving docks.

In his 1979 magazine article, J.P. Neale suggests Ketchum got the inspiration for his ship railway from a paper read to the Institution of Civil Engineers by Edwin Clark in 1866. But in the same letter, Ketchum notes only that Clark provided the design for a hydraulic ship lift for Brunlees' Suez railway.

Brunlees' input was to play a major part in the development of Ketchum's design, and the English engineer's expertise in the technology was later sought by Eads, when he proposed his Mexican ship railway to the U.S. Congress. Eads' plan was, like that of Brunlees, an alternative to another waterway, and like Brunlees, his invention was passed over when the U.S. government backed the construction of the Panama Canal.

Whether or not his introduction to Brunlees' scheme fired a spark within Ketchum at the first moment, it would be 20 years before his design could become reality, and there were other personal and professional challenges awaiting him. By 1865 Ketchum was back home in New Brunswick and was appointed resident engineer on the construction of the railway from Amherst to Moncton. This stretch of track would later become part of the Intercolonial Railway system, and in addition to making Ketchum familiar with the Chignecto Isthmus, would also introduce him to the financial pitfalls that often plagued railway builders of the time.

After the International Contract Company — which had been responsible for that section of the line — failed, Ketchum reached an agreement with Clarke, Punchard & Co. to complete the line as far as Dorchester, N.B. In this regard Ketchum was not unlike another of Canada's great railway builders, Sir Sanford Flemming, who as chief engineer on the Intercolonial as it extended from Truro to Amherst, quit his job to ensure he could complete the line from Truro to Pictou on time, and at a profit to himself. Being his own boss on the Dorchester project quickly brought Ketchum face-to-face with the everyday problems of meeting engineering and financial deadlines.

Some of the blame for the excessive expense of the Dorchester section of the Intercolonial lies with Father of Confederation, E.B. Chandler. One of the New Brunswick participants in the negotiations leading to the creation of Canada, Chandler was to become one of the four men who formed the first board of commissioners for the Intercolonial Railway. This placed him in a classic conflict of interest, but one of which he instantly took advantage, by having the line between Amherst and Moncton swing miles out of its logical path and close to Dorchester.

Ketchum all the while kept close tabs on the project, and demanded exacting work from his managers. After one of his inspections prior to leaving for England, he warned his assistant John Otty by letter Oct. 1 1867: "Do not waste any material from cuttings, that shows bad engineering ... Doherty's work must be dressed off, it looks disgraceful." This Scots-like thrift went with Ketchum to the New Brunswick Railway in 1869, where he was in charge of building the 170-mile line from Fredericton to Edmundston, and to his short term on the Quebec & New Brunswick Railway some years later. His letters to Otty from the Langham Hotel in London's Portland Place, illustrate the severity with which Ketchum undertook his projects:

> Jan. 30 1869
> I do not understand why Green did not work by the mile. It looks as if he took no interest. If he does anything wrong I give you full authority to sack him.
>
> Feb. 20 1869
> I observe you have got Mahoney on again. I hope it is PIECE work. At day work he will not pay."

As for his financial managers, Ketchum was equally ruthless. Writing to Otty about one of his staff, he observed of one offender:

> He has been allowed too much latitude by me which he shall not be indulged again, and when I return I shall be far more strict with him. If he saw the way accountants are obliged to balance here it would be a

good lesson to him.

Certainly, Ketchum was the epitome of a tightwad when his own money was at stake:

> 13 March 1869
> You must stand up to Grant and Boxall in everything. We must show them we can be as strict as they can be. They are trying to cheat me. I should judge by their conduct and my solicitor has valiantly tried to bring them to terms.

Upon being advised to sue the offending party, he told Otty,

> I will want a day or two before deciding this. I do not intend to suspend the works at all events, so long as they may be profitable to me ... Discontinue any work that does not pay a profit — do not increase the force of men — use your discretion, but when I give you this hint — that I am in trouble with Clark and Punchard, I am sure you will act with prudence, but keep it PRIVATE.

Ketchum's correspondence shows he was no mere wild-eyed dreamer, nor was he so totally out of his depth when it came to financial matters, as C.R. MacKay's analysis suggests. Ketchum was not the kind of man who played fast and loose with other people's money. When he took over the contract for the Amherst-Moncton stretch of the Intercolonial Railway, Ketchum paid the liabilities of the International Contract Company out of his own pocket.

He then became the subcontractor for the English firm of Clarke, Punchard & Co. According to Milner,

> After nearly completing this work he had differences with the contractors as to payment, when he obtained an injunction from the supreme court arresting their operations. There was at this time much opposition at

27

Ottawa against the adoption of this section of the ICR, which induced Mr. Ketchum to settle for a large payment in cash, but which was only a small part of his claim.

Putting this money to immediate use, Ketchum paid for the survey of a narrow gauge line from Marysville, N.B. to Quebec. This brought him into the world of Alexander "Boss" Gibson, the lumber baron of Nashwaak County, and whose cotton mill in Marysville was at the time the second largest factory in the country. Milner's history notes:

> A company was incorporated (in 1870) in Fredericton. The government subsidized it to the extent of 10,000 acres of forest land per mile. The company authorized Mr. Ketchum to proceed to England to obtain the money necessary for its construction. He went there and soon after he had made preliminary arrangements, in picking up a home paper, he learned the company had behind his back made arrangements for local parties to furnish the capital and proceed with the work.

The "local parties" included Gibson and Senator J.B. Snowball, with whom Gibson would later ally himself to build the Canada Eastern Railway between Fredericton and Chatham, N.B. Milner suggests it was then that Ketchum learned,

> ... That 10,000 acres timberland to the mile was too great a temptation to the lumbermen in the corporation; they wanted the timber, railway or no railway. The Quebec end of the line was dropped and the road became a local one only .... After all, nobody realized any profits from the huge grants. The richest one died a pensioner, others in the deal did not appear to have benefited by it.

Gibson would later sell his shares in the narrow gauge line when he failed to convince the board of directors of the advantages of converting it to standard gauge. But in many respects he demonstrated he was not the kind of man with whom one trifled. Gibson and Snowball often failed to see-eye-to-eye, and legend has it that when, at one of the annual company meetings, Senator Snowball was voted into the presidency, replacing Gibson, Gibson vowed never to use his own railway. For the following year he shipped every last bail of cotton from his Marysville mill to Fredericton by horse and dray. In order to end the dispute, and no doubt cut his losses incurred by Gibson's boycott, Snowball was obliged to sell his holdings to Gibson.

Clearly, in dealing with such men, Ketchum came to understand how the railway game was played in Canada at the time. With most of the engineering on Gibson's line complete by 1875, Ketchum had moved on, setting himself up in a private consulting practice in Fredericton. It was his dealings with various suppliers and contractors that invariably took Ketchum to the city of Saint John, N.B. While Fredericton was the legislative center of the province, Saint John was the economic heart, and by the mid-19th century the port had become one of the most prosperous on the continent, a rival to Halifax. According to Ketchum's own account:

> The late Mr. John Woodward of St. John, was the first to propose a Marine Railway across the Isthmus of Chignecto. His proposition was designed, however, only for small vessels — not larger than schooners — and there were to be marine slips at each end to haul up vessels out of the water to the level of the land.

Woodward was typical of the businessmen in Saint John at the time. They were a chauvinistic group of entrepreneurs who were convinced of their city's geographical superiority and logistical ability to be the major port on Canada's east coast. It was this kind of economic jingoism which was to give rise to one of the more popular misconceptions about the failure of the ship railway: that it was sabotaged at the federal level by Halifax merchants who saw their position threatened.

The Halifax "conspiracy theory" has been kept alive by those who C.R. MacKay would call the "romanticists" of the railway. Among the leading romantics is David E. Stephens. In his 1972 book *Iron Roads: Railways of Nova Scotia*, Stephens claims, without substantiation, that it was the Halifax shipping industry which finished the railway off:

> As the railway neared completion, the owners of the shipping companies became afraid they would loose (sic) a great deal of revenue due to the loss of the 500 sea miles. To protest the completion of the line, they made a trip to Ottawa, where they were able to persuade the government to cancel its subsidy.

In fact, Ketchum went out of his way to assure the bigger shipping interests he was not after Cunard's liners, or the transatlantic vessels that called on Halifax.

Other romanticists would expand upon the mythology by suggesting Ketchum was attempting deceit, since the age of the smaller wooden vessel he was hoping to attract to the railway had long since passed, leaving the Halifax vessels as his only logical customers. This was not so, however, for although iron and steel-hulled ships had come into their own long before the advent of the ship railway, Nova Scotia was still producing wooden ships of great size.

In *Wooden Ships and Iron Men*, F.W. Wallace notes the head of the Bay of Fundy, where the Fort Lawrence dock was located, was producing ships like the *Fred E. Scammell* (1350 tons) at Eatonville, N.S. in 1880, and the *E.J. Spicer* (1208 tons) at Spencer's Island. All around the Nova Scotia shore — River John, Windsor, Yarmouth, and especially the Parrsboro area, ship builders were producing barkentines and clippers for both the coastal trade, transatlantic runs and the Caribbean. The production continued well into the mid 1880s, long after the St. Lawrence wood boat building trade had died. In any event, neither the Saint John capitalists, nor Ketchum, made any bones about the benefit the railway would provide to the city. Ketchum would openly boast:

> The open winter port of St. John N.B. would naturally become the depot of all tropical products which would be forwarded as returned cargoes in exchange for the manufactures and productions of the Western Provinces of the Dominion.

He went so far as to describe St. John as "an emporium" for the West Indies trade. Whether this was a ploy on Ketchum's part to get the Saint John mercantile interests lobbying on his behalf may never be known. But history, and the records of the Saint John Board of Trade, indicate many people shared his vision. In October of 1883, the board of trade had adopted a resolution supporting Ketchum's plan, which he had begun to unveil earlier in a series of letters in the *Saint John Daily Telegraph*.

By 1875 he had completed his blueprints, which were received with so much interest in the city's Mechanic's and Manufacturer's Exhibition of that year, that the *Telegraph* later displayed them in its newsroom offices for two years after that. Even later, at the fall exhibition of 1890, Ketchum would be amazing Saint John audiences with his miniature working model. The *Dominion Illustrated* of May 1891 would report:

> The lifting docks, the railway and all were there in miniature, and under the manipulation of a skilled attendant, or of Mr. Ketchum himself, the model ship was almost constantly being hoisted up, run across the supposed isthmus and lowered down on the other side.

The newspaper's involvement in the promotion of the railway dispels another popular myth about the railway's demise: that it was doomed from the start by opposition from Liberals. While it is true the Liberal government of Sir Wilfred Laurier sounded the death knell for the Chignecto railway, other Liberals supported it. This was especially true in Saint John, where Liberal and Conservative businessmen frequently set aside their political differences when it seemed they might interfere with the common goal of making a profit.

The *Daily Telegraph* was typical of this sociable arrangement. Politically Liberal, with a large circulation among Conservatives, the *Telegraph* was founded in 1862. Until his death in 1888 William Elder published the *Telegraph*, with noted New Brunswick historian James Hannay as associate editor. Elder was among the original members of the early Chignecto Marine Transport Railway Co. formed after the federal government agreed to back the project. These two men were to offer Ketchum an invaluable resource in their newspaper, allowing him a great deal of space to outline his plan, and to respond to the criticism which ensued.

On April 5 1875, the *Telegraph* published the first of Ketchum's letters in which he proposed, then expanded on his plan to build the ship railway. The letters illustrate both his firm conviction of the success of his invention, and the logic of his argument in its support. They also show how his plans were developing even after his blueprints had been shown at the exhibition. His first version called for three rows of track, later pared down to two.

The fourth and final letter gives a hint as to Ketchum's philosophy of life, and his role as an engineer in the cause of advancing civilization:

> Every opportunity has been given to the public and to engineers to find fault with it if they could. After all this publicity, the worst that has been said is that it is "a novelty" and "an experiment". I think it deserves no such appellation; but let me say that if nothing were to be attempted that had "never been done before" the world would be at a stand still; there would be an end

to all progress. We should never have been civilized, but simply remained in our original savage state.

He closed by saying, rather grandly:

I will refrain, however, from making comparison with the Canal; that scheme is dead and buried. *Requiescat in pace.* Let us erect on its grave a monument of engineering skill and commercial enterprise more worthy of the nineteenth century.

Some of Ketchum's detractors have used these words to support the argument that he was more than just a dreamer, that he was an egotist willing to recklessly commit public and private money to building a monument to himself. Others have suggested, and it is probably more in keeping with his character, that he was referring to a monument to the likes of men he admired the most, Brunlees and Clark.

Another argument to debunk the "egotist" label is that Ketchum made no secret of the contribution made by men like Brunlees, Clark and Baker. From his pamphlets promoting the project it is clear Ketchum was quite comfortable with the title "joint engineer", which he shared with Baker. Be that as it may, Ketchum was soon to find he had to contend with more than the skeptical minds of mere men, for in 1877 the first of two disasters would occur which added weight to the romantic notion that the railway was doomed.

On Wednesday, 20 June fire broke out in the Fairweather's storehouse on the south side of York Point Slip. Fanned by a strong north-east wind, the fire skipped easily through the York Point district, consuming the buildings on Hare's Wharf and sweeping up Smythe Street, along Drury Lane, Mill and Dock Streets. At its peak, the flames of the great Saint John fire could be seen from as far away as Moncton and Fredericton. Even if Ketchum could have seen them from his home in the province's capital, he would never have guessed that by the following morning the offices of the *Daily Telegraph* would be destroyed and his complete linen-drawn plans for the Chignecto Ship Railway, would lie amid the ashes.

It is possible that the fire delayed the development of the Ship Railway by as much as 10 years. This would have serious political and financial ramifications. As will be seen later, the project was now set on a course which would mean that the time when the company's financial need was greatest would coincide with an international monetary crisis.

As if that wasn't enough, the unseen hand of fate would strike again, nine years later on March 14 1886, when the British Cunard liner S.S. *Oregon* sank 18 miles east of Long Island after a collision with the North German Lloyd schooner *Fulda*. All 852 people on board were rescued, but when the *Oregon* went down, she took with her in the purser's safe, the contract between the Chignecto Marine Transport Railway Co. and the Canadian government.

The papers, which had been signed in London by the company's board of directors, were recovered by divers and sped to Ottawa where, still damp and somewhat stained, they were signed by the politicians that May.

Three

The Company Will Satisfy the Government

On May 15 1881, Henry Ketchum launched his plan to bring the Chignecto ship railway into the realm of the possible, with a letter to Sir Charles Tupper in Ottawa. This opening gambit was enhanced by a set of happy circumstances for Ketchum. Tupper was Prime Minister Sir John A. Macdonald's right hand man, the Minister of Canals and Railways, and as luck would have it, the Member of Parliament for Cumberland, in whose bailiwick the railway would be built.

The letter, accompanied by the plans, copies of his four letters in the *Daily Telegraph* and other supporting documents would have made for heavy reading to any unsuspecting recipient. However Ketchum could probably have reassured himself with the notion that Tupper already knew what was afoot, for nothing ever happened in Cumberland County of which the good doctor was not aware. The redoubtable "Cumberland Warhorse" was, after all, one of Canada's leading railway builders, even if he had never so much as lifted a spike-driving hammer. Tupper's role was that of making such grand railway projects as the Canadian Pacific, politically possible.

Born in Amherst in 1821, Tupper was very much a man of his age, when railways and politics were inextricably linked in the Canadian way of life. His successful medical career ended in 1855, when he unseated popular Reform candidate Joseph Howe in his home riding and served in the cabinet as provincial secretary. He became premier of the province in 1864, and his involvement in the operation of the Nova Scotia Railway (begun in 1854 and extended in 1867 from Truro to Pictou) stood him in good stead when he finally entered the Macdonald cabinet in 1870 (he had first been elected federally in 1867), although he did not get the Ministry of Railways and Canals post until 1878. As was typical at the time, although he was a Conservative, Tupper espoused the politics of railways; anyone who supported railways (as a senator once pronounced at the time) got his support.

In his first letter to Tupper, Ketchum noted he was presenting the plans "officially," an indication perhaps that he and Sir Charles had discussed the matter informally at an earlier date. If Ketchum had expected an immediate and positive reply, however, he was disappointed. On Aug. 12 1881, A.P. Bradley, acting secretary of the Department of Railways and Canals wrote back to say quite simply:

> Sir — I am instructed to acknowledge the receipt of a pamphlet entitled "The Cost, Feasibility and Advantages of a ship railway across the Isthmus of Chignecto" and to state that it will receive consideration.

In fact Tupper had turned Ketchum's documents over to his chief engineer, the renowned Collingwood Schreiber. In the meantime, Ketchum fleshed out his plan, and arguments in support of the Ship Railway, in a second letter written Nov. 1 of that year.

The second letter is perhaps the more significant of the two, since for the first time, Ketchum puts a figure on the subsidy needed from the federal government. Tupper was told the estimated total cost of the ship railway was about four million dollars. (In fact, the total cost would have been closer to five million.) Ketchum told Tupper, "the company will look to the Government for a guarantee of interest, or a subsidy for a term of twenty years. The Company will provide security for the due performance of the work, and to guarantee the safety of vessels transported." Then Ketchum went on to make boast which would later prove to be fatal for the project:

> The Company will satisfy the Government by practical demonstration of the safe transport over one mile of ship railway of a steamer of 1,000 tons burthen, and by raising and lowering said steamer in the hydraulic lifts in full cargo before receiving from the government an installment of subsidy.

By imposing this restriction on himself, making it a condition of receiving the subsidy, Ketchum would later make it impossible for the Chignecto Marine Transport Railway Co. to get cash from the federal coffers when financing was desperately needed. The gesture was in the tradition of many engineers of the time, particularly men like J.B. Eads, who often undertook to finish projects using their own money before being reimbursed by government. The ability to deliver on these promises was a point of professional honor for engineers of the age.

Also in the second letter, Ketchum suggested a subsidy of $200,000 per year for 20 years would be reasonable. He planned to raise his capital through the formation of a company, the CMTR, under a federal charter. The company would build, operate and maintain the system, charging tolls for the transportation of ships and later for the transportation of passengers to the Prince Edward Island ferry terminal at Cape Tormentine, N.B.

This second scheme is one of the lesser-known facets of Ketchum's project, and was later dropped without much explanation, although in his second letter Ketchum began to make a strong case for his company's operation of the rail link. He was quick to point out to Tupper the island railway proposal was by no means an admission that the ship railway faced a possibility of failure.

The Tormentine rail link was to become the property of Josiah Wood, a prominent Sackville, N.B. merchant and politician, who sat as the Conservative MP for Westmorland from 1882-1895. It was during this time that Wood secured the federal subsidy for his railway which was completed in 1886, leading some to suspect part of Ketchum's plan had been hijacked by a political opportunist. In fact, Wood supported Ketchum's scheme, even to the point of writing to the government (while still an MP for the Chignecto region) in August of 1889, in support of yet another of Ketchum's pleas for changes in the terms of the subsidy agreement.

One of the enduring myths of the Chignecto Ship Railway holds that Ketchum's grand plan was constantly thwarted by politicians, but Ketchum was not above playing the political game either. His company was comprised of several leading politicians. Listed among his associates were Edwin Clark (the British engineer who masterminded the hydraulic lift technology), Thomas C. Keefer, Charles R. Coker, R.G. Lunt, William Elder (the Saint John newspaper editor and publisher), New Brunswick MPP Charles C. Gregory, Col. Charles J. Stewart, Christopher Milner, the Hon. P.A. Landry, J.C. Brundage, W.C. Milner, W.H. Marston, Hon. J.S. Carswell, Hon. A.W. Ogilvie, John H. Parks, A.E. Killam MPP, James S. Hickman and W.D. Douglas Main.

The involvement of the Milners was the result of a family connection. While still working on the Dorchester section of the Intercolonial, Ketchum (whose residence was listed as Dorchester at the time) had met, and subsequently on August 21 1886, married Sarah Elizabeth Milner, a resident of Sackville. The Milners were an influential and respected family in the Tantramar region (as the New Brunswick side of the border with Nova Scotia is known.)

W.C. Milner was a notable local historian, who is believed to be the first of many to attach nefarious political motives to the ultimate failure of the railway. It is from Milner's papers that latter-day historians have nurtured the romantic versions of the ship railway saga. His description of the ultimate political abandonment of the project set the tone for others:

> During the year (this was Milner's version of the resumption of work after a financial crisis had interrupted construction) the charter of the Company expired. The Company being then in a position to resume work, applied to the Government to extend the charter. The answer of the leader of the Government was astounding to the company. "We will renew the charter if you will drop the subsidy." This was a shock to the investors — vicious as it was unexpected. When they put four millions of dollars in it, they never dreamed that its security as an investment would be suddenly swept away on the word of a Nova Scotia attorney, in violation of all precedents.

Just who the "Nova Scotia attorney" was, Milner doesn't make clear, although it could have been the prime minister of the day, Sir John Thompson. We are, however, getting ahead of the history.

All the original supporters of the Ship Railway Company were later to fade from the scene, but one of the more interesting members of the group was the Honorable C.J. Townshend, then the Liberal-Conservative MLA for Cumberland County. The Amherst lawyer would replace Tupper as MP for Cumberland when Tupper went to England to serve as Canada's High Commissioner. This put Townshend in Parliament at an equally opportune time for the ship railway company.

At this point it must be noted that C.R. MacKay's history of the failure of the railway offers the best chronology of events that followed, but even then there are gaps. In March of 1880, for example, (but ignored by MacKay) James Buchanan Eads had presented the U.S. Congress with his proposal to build a ship railway across the Tehuantepec isthmus of Mexico, as a cheaper and more efficient alternative to the Panama Canal. For a time there was something of a race on between the two men to be the

39

first to put this new technology into action. Probably because of the Saint John fire, Eads eventually took the lead, but Ketchum made no secret of his admiration for Eads' plan, and in his published version of the presentation to Tupper, he included Brunlees' evaluation of the Tehuantepec project, along with endorsements from a handful of noted engineers.

Unfortunately such a close comparison might have proven fatal for Ketchum's railway. Congress twice defeated bills in support of Eads' venture, choosing instead to build the canal to speed traffic from the east coast of the United States to the west coast. As if to add insult to injury, the Panama Canal was started under a company controlled by Ferdinand Lesseps, the same man who had engineered the construction of the Suez canal — the same canal that was chosen over the Brunlees ship railway!

These arguments would not be raised immediately however. The only tangible objection to Ketchum's plan was raised by bureaucrats who warned that the later revised estimate of $4.3 million would be the bare minimum needed to see the work through.

Tupper's chief engineer, Collingwood Schreiber, was in no doubt. He told Tupper Ketchum's plan was feasible, and as it was estimated at one third the cost of building a canal, indeed practical. This evaluation may have been made hastily. Collingwood Schreiber was a busy man in those days. He had been appointed engineer-in-chief in the wake of Sir Sanford Flemming, and had inherited the task of overseeing the construction of the Canadian Pacific Railway on the government's behalf. Schreiber's approval was probably token in any event, since Tupper was to make it clear in his resolution of May 9 1882 that the engineer-in-chief was merely "consulted."

In light of the fact that Ketchum's was unproven technology, all that Schreiber had to base his opinion on was the massive support Eads would receive from his colleagues for the Tehuantepec ship railway. To a man, these were all enthusiastic supporters of the concept.

Prime Minister Macdonald was another enthusiastic

supporter, and long after the order-in-council was authorized on April 12 1882, he liked to take visitors to Parliament into the Railway Room to show them Ketchum's plans and explain the wondrous concept in great detail.

Four

The Company Was Misled

On May 9, 1882 Tupper took the resolution to approve a subsidy to the Chignecto Marine Transportation Company to the House of Commons, where the political battle was joined. In his analysis, C.R. MacKay calls the first parliamentary debates on the Chignecto scheme short, but "prophetic."

A battle of some sort was imminent. Pierre Berton, in *The National Dream*, notes the depth of the Liberal mistrust of Tory-sponsored railway projects:

> The Liberal opposition to Macdonald's railway policy stemmed in part from the excesses of the railway boom of the fifties ... and they had reason to be outraged. Between 1854 and 1857 an estimated one hundred million dollars in foreign capital was pumped into Canada for the purpose of building railways. Much of it found its way into the pockets of promoters and contractors. The usual scheme was to form a company, keep control of it, float as much stock as possible and then award lush construction contracts to men on the inside.

> Small wonder the party which viewed Macdonald's

transcontinental railway as an act of "insane recklessness" would look dimly upon a plan to take sailing ships over 17 miles of land by train — a plan which by the time of Laurier's election to power had taken almost 15 years to lay about 30 miles of track.

The seeds of mistrust were sown well before Tupper laid the Chignecto Ship Railway plan before the Commons, but his timing couldn't have been worse. On May 9, 1882, the day after he tabled his resolution in support of the subsidy, Hansard records a series of particularly bitter debates on other topics, each destined to have an effect upon the debate of May 11. Having dealt rather promptly with a bill to abolish postage on newspapers, the Commons began to haggle over the details of an increased subsidy to the newly-joined province of Manitoba. The government's case was laid before the house by Sir Leonard Tilley, of Saint John, N.B., who had earned the wrath of the opposition's generals, Alexander Mackenzie and George Blake. Almost immediately Tilley was under fire for his apparent inability to give the house an accounting of how the sum of the increased subsidy was calculated.

Macdonald's cabinet ministers were taken to task for their continued practice of tabling proposals involving major expenditures without giving the opposition time to peruse the figures, or form an opinion. This point was made clear by Mills, the MP for Bothwell who told Sir Leonard:

> In dealing with matters of finance, and in submitting a proposition of this kind (the Manitoba subsidy amendment) which may be approved or not by the House, the members of the Government are acting as agents of Parliament. The advisors of the Crown are nothing more, yet they have ignored Parliament, disregarded its authority, and have simply come down at the last moment and asked its approval of a certain proposal, allowing no time within which an opinion can be formed. What is the position the hon. gentleman

occupies before the House? It is this: he comes down and tells the House that as Minister of the Public Treasury, and as controller of its finances, he makes a certain proposal. He informs the House that a conclusion has been arrived at, but he does not go out of his way to furnish information which would enable hon. members to form an opinion for themselves; but he asks the House not to excuse an independent judgment, but to accept the resolution at which the Government have arrived. This is in perfect accord with the policy of the Government during the past four years. The Ministers have looked on Parliament as a body appointed to register the decrees of the Government, and we find how the Government has treated Parliament. The Government have come down at the end of the Session and submitted a proposition which is to remain a contract between the Dominion Government and the Province of Manitoba for the next ten years. The hon. gentleman knew right well that he thereby ties the hands of his successors in office, and although that is obvious, yet Parliament is called upon to support that proposition without any information having been given. I enter my protest against such a policy. I assumed when I was elected that I was to exercise an independent judgment as to what the public interests required, and I declined to abrogate my functions, and hand over the trust which the electors have committed to me and the Administration. The hon. gentleman must have considered the details of this proposal which he has submitted, and it is necessary that all information should be furnished to the House to enable it to arrive at a proper conclusion; but the hon. gentleman has not done so, and he and his colleagues, who expect the Session to close within a few days, know it is impossible to give a proposition of this kind the consideration to which it is entitled.

While Mr. Mills protested a matter of high principal, one can only imagine the smirks on the faces of

Macdonald's men, who knew not only that the policy was highly effective, but that they would use it again and again.

That same day Parliament was asked to consider a proposal tabled by Sir Hector Langevin to appoint commissioners to oversee the management and improvement of the harbor at Saint John, N.B. The focus of the Liberal opposition this time was that the commissioners were to be in control of $250,000 in government funding, but the federal cabinet ministers could not, or would not, say how the money would be spent.

The third pill to sour the Liberal mood, and it had to be swallowed immediately after the protracted debate over Langevin's resolution, was the government's thwarting of a proposed amendment to a Liberal bill to prevent fraud in connection with public contracts.

Presented by Phillipe Baby Casgrain, the MP for L'Islet, the amendment stipulated:

> That it is not expedient, nor in the interest of the public service, to vote any money for expenditure on public contracts without some adequate measure of legislation to prevent and punish frauds in contracts involving expenditure of public moneys, and that this House regrets that the Ministry did not bring and carry such measures before this Parliament.

Clearly, the Liberals were on a crusade to force some measure of fiscal accountability on the Conservatives, and the Chignecto scheme appears destined to be a casualty of the war.

Tupper's campaign to confound the opposition was continued May 11, after a long debate on the redistribution of seats in the House of Commons. He rose to introduce his bill approving the subsidy to the Chignecto Marine Transportation Co. by acknowledging the lateness of the hour (the first debate had taken all of the afternoon's business to that point) and indicating all members should be thoroughly familiar with the topic anyway:

> ... the subject in one form or another, has so long engaged the attention of Parliament, that I do not think it will be necessary to detain the House very long in explaining the proposal of these resolutions.

But detain them he did, first by going over the history of the ill-fated Baie Verte canal project and referring to the royal commission's report which had placed the canal at the top of its list of priorities. This was hardly likely to stir support from the Liberals, since it was Mackenzie's government that had gone out of its way to repudiate the Allan Commission's findings, and had killed the Baie Verte project outright.

It was Mackenzie who was first into the fray, denying Tupper's assertion that everyone had been kept fully informed of Ketchum's plan:

> I have already complained that we were not aware, when the matter was before that (Railways) Committee, of the intentions of the Government relating to it, and gave it the less attention on that account. Had the hon. gentleman (Tupper) at that time informed the Committee of the full proposal of the government it would have received much more searching criticism than it was proposed by anyone to give it.

Mackenzie noted his party had dismissed the proposal on the basis of the failed plan to build a similar railway from Toronto to Georgian Bay. Mention of this project also dispels the Maritime myth that Ketchum's idea was a new one.

The former prime minister refuted Tupper's claim that there was enough business to support Ketchum's railway, using the findings of his own commission back in 1875:

> I think it was rather conclusively proved that vessels

passing to the West Indies would never seek that route, but that it would be much cheaper and better for them to take a straight line eastward until they reached the open sea and got into a direct line to the West India Islands.

Mackenzie went on to cast further doubt:

> The money no doubt will be raised by the projector, but there is every danger that you may have a repetition of the Grand Trunk experience — a declaration that the work will stop, after the expenditure of the first subsidy, till more assistance be given.

At this point F. Killam, the Liberal MP for Yarmouth, N.S. joined the fight, telling the House it was being asked to approve three million dollars for "an experiment." He went on to castigate Tupper for changing the course of government policy to favor the Chignecto scheme, and while not pretending to understand the engineering, reinforced Mackenzie's arguments about the route's ability to pay for itself.

If the Chignecto railway's initial political problem was a disagreement over practicality and profitability, it would soon change into one of outright suspicion that, as Mackenzie and the Liberals had charged, a boondoggle was afoot to milk the federal coffers. As MacKay notes:

> The relationship between the CMTR (Chignecto Marine Transport Railway Co.) and the Canadian government was to be dominated by that firm's unsuccessful attempts to raise capital and to alter the terms of the initial agreement.

Within a month of Parliament's authorization of the agreement, Ketchum was calling for alterations, having been told two months prior to incorporation that financiers would not handle any bond issues unless the federal government guaranteed interest payments on the capital invested. On Feb. 10 1883, the company petitioned the government for permission to double the capital stock to two million dollars, and asked for an increase in first mortgage bonds. This was agreed to on April 18 1883. But on April 19, Schreiber had told Tupper Ketchum would be asking for yet more changes in the wake of yet more revised estimates.

As MacKay notes: "Before a sod had been turned or a plank laid, a pattern was emerging of recurrent delays attributable to financiers' wariness and inadequate engineering estimates."

This may in part be true, but overlooks the fact that the CMTR estimates were in all likelihood no more or less wildly inaccurate than those of the Intercolonial, Canadian Pacific or any other of the multifarious railways that were springing up across the country, backed by Conservatives and Liberals alike.

Another fact overlooked by MacKay in his evaluation of the engineering estimates is the difficulty presented by the terrain. Although it is almost perfectly flat, and rarely has a point rising more than 50 feet above sea level, the isthmus presented its own challenges, one of which was not unlike that presented to the engineers on the CPR.

At the center of the isthmus, and virtually unknown until the railway began to cross it, lies a huge network of floating bogs. This terrain was much like the muskeg of Northern Ontario, encountered by the CPR's crews, and so vividly described by Berton:

> There were the notorious sinkholes — little lakes over which a thick crust of vegetable matter had formed and into which the line might tumble at any time. There was one sinkhole near Savanne, north of Fort William, so legend has it, where an entire train with a thousand feet of track was swallowed whole. Sometimes new sinkholes would appear in land thought to be as solid as Gibraltar.
>
> A mile from Bonheur, a construction crew believed it had filled a muskeg hole when the entire track

suddenly vanished into the black mud. Trainload after trainload of gravel was dumped into the apparently bottomless pit while men sweated with timbers to shore it up.

It was into the Chignecto bog that Ketchum's men were to drive pile after pile, seeking to create a firm foundation for the rail bed. To the eye, and especially in winter when it was first surveyed by English engineers unfamiliar with the climate, the land looked firm enough — certainly one could walk over it without knowing what lay beneath — and there was probably no way at the time that an engineer could have discovered a bog until the first pile broke through the crust and sank out of sight.

According to local legend, a work crew on the Chignecto project one night left a steam shovel on the site over the bog, only to return the next morning to find it had sunk, completely and irretrievably, into the morass. There was a similar problem at the Fort Lawrence end of the line, created by the mud of the LaPlanche River. *The Dominion Illustrated* reported in 1891: "In making the docks the excavations had to be carried far deeper than at first designed, in order to find solid rock foundations for the masonry."

Typical of the times, however, when man's mastery of nature must have seemed omnipotent, the geography of the region was dismissed by the writers of *The Dominion Illustrated* as insignificant:

> The Isthmus of Chignecto is only seventeen miles wide, the line of the railway is straight across and the heaviest gradient but a fifth of one per cent. But two large cuttings had to be excavated, and one bog filled up. The road is, practically, a dead level. But one stream had to be crossed (the Tidnish), and a single span sufficed. So that, although in a sense difficult, the physical features to be overcome could hardly be called formidable.

What might have spurred the Liberal opposition to the Chignecto scheme was a determination to have a victory over Tupper and Macdonald at any cost, and if that victory could not be the CPR, then the CMTR would serve just as well.

Initial public reaction to the new company's project was not overwhelming, or immediate. By Oct. 14 1882, the *Halifax Herald* was reporting Ketchum's triumphant return from England to announce that the firm of Cutbill & Lungo was considering taking the contract on the project. Engineer Darton Hutton was expected in the region "in the near future" to begin the survey for the firm, which had previously worked on railway projects in India, Brazil and Venezuela, and on the canals of The Netherlands.

Reporting back to Cutbill & Lungo, Hutton wrote of the enterprise positively, and a contract was signed. Cutbill withdrew from the project after little more than a year, and the firm of Morton, Rose & Co., which had initially taken on the CPR contract, politely declined to become involved. The problem would be solved in 1887 by Sir Benjamin Baker, who put Ketchum in contact with the firm of John G. Meiggs & Son., with whom Baker had worked on previous projects.

Local support for the project was immediate. It was later noted in company documents: "The residents and freeholders of the County of Cumberland through which the railway line runs, have, by instrument dated 9th October, 1883, guaranteed to provide all the lands required for the railway and docks, and procure the necessary conveyances for the same free from all charges and expenses to the company."

This gift was not without its strings, however. In his undated Memo respecting Chignecto Ship Railway, which was probably written around 1894, the Tory MP for the area, A.R. Dickey wrote of the "heavy local taxes" paid by the company. The firm would later come to regret accepting the gift. On Aug. 12 1902, the leading director of the company, A.D. Provand, would write to Prime Minister Sir Wilfred Laurier complaining: "The Company was misled into undertaking the enterprise and Cumberland County did their share in misleading us, by giving land to the Company." (This indignation was in reaction to the municipality having informed the company of its intention to have the land returned when work stopped on the site after 1891. Three days after Provand's letter, the CMTR informed Laurier the trustees appointed by the company's shareholders had taken possession of the property.)

On Feb. 26 1884, the company further muddied the waters by requesting that the annual subsidy be raised from $150,000 to $175,000 for 25 years, and began to stretch its credibility by further asking that the government do some of the dredging necessary at both ends of the line on an almost constant basis. In order to keep costs down, Ketchum said, it would also be necessary to admit some of the essential items (like the extra-heavy rails and hydraulic machinery) into the country duty-free.

There followed two more requests, one on Feb. 26 1884 for a further $20,000 annually under the terms of the Dry Dock Act (for each port could be used to effect ship repair in the same manner as a conventional dry dock), the other in June suggesting the subsidy could be set at $187,000 for 20 years if the government found the 25-year-term unacceptable. That Ketchum got less than he asked for, was possibly a reflection of just how far he had pressed his luck, and how sensitive the ship railway had become politically. In the fall of 1885 the government agreed to increase the subsidy to $170,682 for 20 years, but specified that the work must be completed by July 1 1889.

By the time the amendments reached the House of Commons on April 13 1886, J.H. Pope had replaced Tupper as Minister of Railways and Canals, Tupper had gone to England, and C.J. Townshend was the sitting member for Cumberland by virtue of the ensuing byelection. This by no means assured the bill of smooth sailing, for the debate was as stormy as anything the North Atlantic could serve up. The bill did pass, but not before the opponents could force more conditions upon the company, this time stipulating the subsidy would be paid only in such amounts as to realize a 7.5 per cent return on investment. Any profit after that would be put toward repayment of the subsidy. This condition was intended to assure the Liberals the company's intention was not to grab the subsidy money and run, as other railway ventures had done, and would continue to do, and the contract was again signed by the company on April 4, 1886.

Five

A Baby In Its Mother's Arms

It is inevitable that a comparison should be made between Henry Ketchum and James Eads as both made proposals for ship railways. As has been mentioned, for a time there was something of a race on between the two men to put this technology into action. In his first letter to Tupper (see Appendix) Ketchum uses Eads' proposal for a ship railway across the Isthmus of Tehuantepec to support his argument for the feasibility of his Chignecto project.

James Buchanan Eads was as enigmatic and flamboyant as any of the great men of his age. Recognized as one of the outstanding engineers of the 19th century, he constantly sought to crown each success with yet another monumental undertaking. His ship railway represents his only failure.

He was born in Lawrenceburg, Indiana, May 23 1820, a distant relative (his mother's cousin) to James Buchanan, then a junior Pennsylvania congressman who went on to become President of the United States. This by no means guaranteed Eads a privileged life, for his father, never very successful in business, took the family from Cincinnati, to Louisville and finally St. Louis in search of their share of the American dream.

Young James had little chance for a formal education in

his early years, a shortcoming he was determined to make up in the library of his first employer, a benevolent St. Louis dry goods merchant who allowed the young stock clerk to devour the information contained in the books ... on his own time.

In search of greater things Eads became purser on a Mississippi river boat at the age of 18, and soon began putting his mind to work on the task of salvaging cargo from the depths of the muddy river. The waterway was one of the principal commercial routes of the United States, superseded only by the growing railroad network, and although it was a river, it was capable of storms to equal any marine maelstrom. Eads' solution to the salvage problem, devised at age 22, was to construct a boat he called a "submarine." It was actually more of a diving tender, remaining on the surface while a diver in a bell Eads designed, walked along the river bottom.

He made his fortune over the next 12 years, retrieving pig iron, lead ingots and other valuable freight that had gone overboard and had been otherwise written off by its owners. He retired briefly, to marry, settle down, and start a glass manufacturing enterprise that was ruined by the Mexican War. Undaunted, he returned to the salvage business, building three more submarines, and within a few years, operating a fleet of ten boats.

With the onset of the Civil War, Eads turned his attention to national security; he recognized control of the Mississippi River system would be an important key to a Union victory. His next bold measure was to propose that he build a flotilla of shallow-draft steam-powered ironclads to patrol the river. The proposal met with some reluctance from Congress, but true to his nature Eads delivered the boats on time, employing 4,000 men working day and night shifts seven days a week.

The vessels would become the first ironclads to fight in North America, and the first in the world to engage enemy ships, spearheading General Ulysses S. Grant's thrusts against Fort Henry and Fort Donelson, the first major Union victories in the war. The boats would also later be used successfully by Andrew Foote and David Farragut, fighting all the way down the river through Memphis and out into Mobile Bay.

This achievement earned Eads first consideration when it came to selecting someone to oversee the construction of a bridge across the Mississippi at St. Louis, even though there were other eminent, and formally educated, engineers qualified for the challenge. On Aug. 20 1867, using his knowledge of the river, his own self-taught education and what he had learned of iron and steel fabrication from his salvage and wartime ventures Eads began construction of the steel triple-arched bridge.

At this time Eads consulted Benjamin Baker, the young English engineer who had developed a certain expertise in long span bridge construction. There was no doubt Baker's input was needed. The three spans of Eads' bridge were 502, 520 and 502 feet respectively, of triangular-braced 18-inch hollow steel tubes set in piers based on bedrock.

Reaching the bedrock posed a major problem, since it lay some 100 feet below the surface of the mighty Mississippi, but Eads adapted his diving bell technology of twenty years earlier to place men beneath the water digging mud and breathing compressed air. Two workers died (March 19 1870), and many others contracted what was then called caisson disease (now called the bends), until Eads built a hospital ship to provide better nutrition (at least for the river bed diggers), and demanded slow decompression for the workers as they came off their shifts.

Eads was exacting in his standards, in a style adopted by Henry Ketchum, and was not above returning steel, (much of it supplied by wealthy industrialist Andrew Carnegie) on the grounds that it was not suitable for the project. Carnegie's mills were often forced to roll the same piece of steel as many as three times before Eads deemed it to have reached the acceptable strength of 60,000 pounds to the square inch.

Although the construction of bridges across the river was destined to decimate the traffic up and down the

Mississippi, Eads was obliged to build his bridge without interrupting the riverboats; this posed yet another challenge for him.

Using Baker's imported cantilever technology, and timber beams rather than the more conventional cranes mounted on boats, Eads proposed to maneouvre the arches out over the river on cables, with the top halves of each arch held back over the piers. To connect the two halves of the center arch, Eads' assistant, Col. Henry Flad planned to bend the span slightly until it was between the ends of the arch on each side, then remove the cantilever support, in effect allowing the arches to spring back into shape and firm the joint.

Meanwhile, Eads devised a second plan; he would use a wrought-iron threaded plug, to close the distance between the two ends of the other spans, which he would shorten by five inches.

Flad was foiled by an unusual September warm spell, which caused the arches at the north of the bridge to warp. When ice packs failed to correct the expansion problem, the engineers moved to Eads' Plan B, and closed the first arch on Sept. 17 1873.

The finished bridge, which opened July 4 1874, immediately became a wonder of the modern world, the largest of any bridge built up to that time. Soon after, in search of new conquests, Eads got involved in the plan to provide year-round navigation at New Orleans, at the mouth of his beloved river.

As with the bridge, skeptics doubted it could be done, but despite problems with sediment and the cantankerous currents of the river, Eads succeeded. He took only five years to create a practical channel, built on time, on budget and at his own expense, to be reimbursed later upon the successful conclusion of the scheme. This practice, which was remarkably similar to the offer Ketchum would make in his initial letters to Sir Charles Tupper, would also be used by Eads to promote the Tehuantepec ship railway.

Construction of a canal bridging the narrow isthmus between the Atlantic and the Pacific had occupied the minds of many since the Spaniard Cortez first crossed the region in 1520. In Eads' time, the governments of both Great Britain and the United States had, on numerous occasions since the mid-1800s, entertained various schemes for crossing the isthmus, where the Mexican Sierras reach a height of a mere 700 feet on the Pacific side. The rationale was obvious: the hazards of sailing round Cape Horn were identical to those of the voyage around the tip of Africa. Eads had also a far more pragmatic goal. The California gold rush of 1849 spurred a race among merchants in the eastern U.S. to be the first to supply the hungry gold camps. In those days eggs commonly sold for a dollar apiece, and a staple like a sack of flour cost a sourdough $100. The competition was fierce, but either route — overland through Indian country, or by sea via Cape Horn — was dangerous and slow.

The quickest time made by any vessel from New York to San Francisco was 89 days and eight hours (a record yet to be eclipsed by modern vessels) clocked by the California clipper *Flying Cloud*, launched at East Boston in 1851.

Even in that short time, the voyage was brutal. While smaller coastal vessels could traverse the Isthmus of Panama (various lines were carrying lesser cargo across the 50-mile isthmus between 1848 and 1869, when the transcontinental railway route opened) the toll on both ships and crew was merciless. Even using the shorter route, the voyage took three months through mosquito-infested waters in relentless heat and humidity. The pay had to be high to attract seasoned sailors, the insurance rates were astronomical.

In 1850 the Bulwer-Clayton treaty between the U.S. and Britain paved the way for recognition of who would control the route, a question not to be fully settled until 1903, when the Republic of Panama granted the U.S. the right to occupy the ten-mile wide zone in perpetuity.

Ferdinand de Lesseps' initial design of 1879 proposed a canal that would run from cost to coast on the same level, but he failed to take into account the tropical floods of the Chagres River, which forced the use of locks to control the water levels.

Eads took his proposal for a ship railway before Congress in April of 1880. He told the lawmakers his scheme would cost one half of what it would take to build a canal with locks, one quarter the cost of a canal at tide level, in a third or a quarter of the time:

> And that, when built, ships of the maximum tonnage can be moved with safety, at four or five times greater speed than in a canal; that a greater number of vessels per day can be transported than by canal; that the capacity of a ship railway can be easily increased to meet the demands of commerce; that the cost of maintenance would be much less than that of a canal, and that a railway can be constructed and operated in places where it is not practicable to construct a canal.

Eads' involvement in ship railways should have provided more than enough argument to support the feasibility of Ketchum's proposal for the CMTR. Sir Charles Tupper referred to the American plan in his May 11 1882 address in the House of Commons:

> I have the most ample evidence and testimony of the most eminent engineers in the world of the entire practicability of the scheme; and were I submitting this as a Government work, I would feel justified in detaining the House while I read from these authorities. The Congress of the United States have examined the question thoroughly and express their entire confidence in the possibility of carrying ships up greater inclines and for longer distances than is proposed here, and Congress are prepared to expend a large sum of public money to accomplish a similar work in another place.

This of course was not particularly true, but Tupper was never one to let fact get in the way of political fancy. There was, however, a certain amount of interest in the

United States in the Chignecto scheme. Several U.S. engineers who would be called before Congress, and a few senators who would be asking them questions, approached Ottawa at various times seeking details on Ketchum's ship railway.

The Eads plan was similar to Brunlees', with a few exceptions, the first being that on the Eads railway, the ships would be hauled out of the water on an incline, a real marine slip, 300 feet long and 30 feet deep:

> The ship is to be fitted into a cradle and kept in place by blocks six or ten feet apart. The railway is to consist of twelve rails of the ordinary width, the wheels under the cradle to be at three feet distance from each other and to bear a pressure of five tons, the average pressure on the driving wheels of the freight locomotives being six and a half tons while at rest.

But, as with Ketchum, there was immediate doubt about the plan, and more particularly about the ability of a ship to withstand the pressure of being taken out of the water fully-laden. Ketchum's initial papers to Tupper described the situation thus:

> He (Eads) replied that any vessel that was built and was fit to be passed by underwriters, and was thought capable of withstanding the gales and hurricanes of the Atlantic and Pacific Oceans, was capable of being carried on the railway with absolute safety; indeed, with as much safety as a baby in its mother's arms.

This would have been a much bigger railway than that planned by Ketchum. For one thing, it would cross a much rougher terrain, and would require, by Brunlees' own estimate, four to ten locomotives, each equipped with two toothed wheels to grip a rack laid along the railway. Brunlees advocated using Clark's hydraulic lift, but Eads dropped that particular apparatus.

The close involvement of Brunlees and Clark in both

Eads' and Ketchum's schemes might cause one to suspect that somehow these two gentlemen, having been thoroughly rebuffed upon presenting their brainchild originally to the French, were constantly seeking other people to build their ship railway, and thus prove their genius.

(This scenario seems to fit a pattern that is typical of the history of Maritime Canada's industrial development: Foreign investors use government guarantees (like subsidies or outright grants and loans) to float their fledgling projects while local people are used to "front" the operation. The history of all three Maritime provinces is littered with examples and some spectacular failures; Bricklin, Clairtone and the like. Chignecto could well have been one of the earliest examples of this trend.)

There could be some validity to this idea, but other engineers, many with nothing to gain by backing the Ead's proposal, did so enthusiastically, including the likes of E.J. Reed, then chief constructor for the British Royal Navy, and a host of U.S. naval engineers and experts, all of whom testified to Congress either orally, or in letters of support (including the faithful Henry Flad, who was then president of the Board of Public Works in St. Louis.) This overwhelming volume of evidence (much of it quoted by Ketchum in his presentation to Tupper) did nothing, however, to sway the politics of the decision, as refusal of Congress to back the Tehuantepec ship railway, not once, but twice, clearly shows.

Six

A Hopeless Task

By Ketchum's own estimates the Chignecto Marine Transport Railway would earn $270,000 per year, which he detailed in his pamphlet of 1884. The booklet was published in London, serving as a prospectus for investors, but it was merely an updated copy of the original pamphlet he had included in the documents sent to Tupper in 1881.

Quoting a variety of sources, Ketchum contended there were enough ships plying the route to ensure the railway would entice a healthy share to its more advantageous passage.

> Of this total (national) tonnage indicated by the entries and clearances, there were 6,321,610 tons, particularly belonging to the Maritime Provinces, including Quebec, New Brunswick, Nova Scotia and Prince Edward Island.

Ketchum felt his railway could expect as much as 10 per cent of that traffic, about 600,000 tons, a figure critics such as MacKay have used to back the argument there was no concrete basis on which to estimate the commercial success of the venture. This criticism overlooks the fact that, even today, business forecasts are based upon best guesses and hunches, and in Ketchum's case it was not unreasonable to suppose 600 captains would want to cut short their trips between Boston and Montreal via the Chignecto route.

Ketchum concluded a fair rate for use of the line, per ship, would be 50 cents per ton on the cargo, and 10 cents per ton on the hull. The 600,000 tons, at 60 cents, would therefore generate $360,000 in revenue on the line. Since there was no loading or unloading of cargo, no station expenses and relatively little maintenance to be done on the line (since it was "so substantially built that repair and maintenance will be light"): "The cost, therefore of working will be but little more than inexpensive maintenance and locomotive power, added to the cost of lifting and depositing vessels from and to the docks," he noted in his prospectus.

Ketchum quoted the English ratio of cost of locomotive power to gross earnings at 17.5 per cent, and added his own experience from his days on the ICR to arrive at the actual cost of that power at .25 cents per ton per mile: "Assuming the gross weight on the ship railway is to be double the paying freight; which is an unfavorable comparison, as before shown — the foregoing results of working an ordinary railway in the country shows that it costs for locomotive power one-half cent per ton per mile, or, one farthing English money — which is equal to 8 1/2 cents or 4d. per ton for the whole transportation of 17 miles."

His detailed examination drew to a swift conclusion. Ketchum estimated it would cost approximately $36 to operate one lift with one vessel on it, or $72 for one transit. By comparison, his estimate on the cost of maintenance was brief, suggesting all office and other expenses would come to no more than $5 per day, or an additional 1 1/2 cents per ton: "Total for 17 miles, 6d. per tone, which is exactly twenty-five per cent of the receipts on the cargoes." That 25 per cent translated into an annual operating expense of $90,000 according to Ketchum. But it was this mathematics which led later analysts to conclude the railway would not be feasible, first because there was no guarantee of the business volume, and secondly because his labor and maintenance costs were too low.

Obviously Ketchum did not intend the operation of the railway to be labor-intensive. It seems clear that beyond the wages of engineers and firemen for the locomotives, engineers in the lifthouses and perhaps an agent or two to watch the bookkeeping, the ships were expected to supply their own labor in blocking the ship and stabilizing it with the cradle before the crossing.

Ketchum did make allowances for his estimate of the traffic volume, noting the firm's first priority would be: "To encourage and develop non-existent trade by low rates at first until the railway is worked up to its full capacity." The company also planned to generate repeat business by offering special rates for steamers on a regular run, and in any event, "to compete with freights around Nova Scotia."

Ketchum's most significant oversight, however, may have been in his underestimation of the time the company would have in which to operate. Even before construction of the Canso Causeway in the 1950s began to further increase ice jams, the upper Bay of Fundy and more especially the Northumberland Strait, between Nova Scotia and Prince Edward Island, were often impassable, because of ice, between November and May. This would leave the railway a season of just five months in which to carry 600 ships, or 120 ships a month, four ships per day.

With the crossing alone expected to take about two hours, and assuming another ship was waiting at either end (to avoid what is commonly called a deadhead run, or a trip with no revenue cargo) the railway would have to have been a 24-hour operation with absolutely no "down time" including delays for whatever minor repairs Ketchum had anticipated.

He had acknowledged the possibility of a winter shutdown in his proposal to Tupper, but his original plan noted the railway would operate in winter as part of his link to the P.E.I. ferry. How he planned to supplement the line's income after the P.E.I. link was dropped in favor of Woods' railway, is not clear.

The Isthmus of Chignecto is one of those places in possession of its own peculiar climate. This should come as no surprise. Trapped between two large bodies of water of different temperature (the Northumberland Strait claims the warmest waters north of the Carolinas; the Bay of Fundy is considerably cooler) the isthmus is almost constantly buffeted by unimpeded and unpredictable winds. Taking water from either side, these winds can drench the isthmus with rain even when the surrounding region is enjoying sunshine. So it was as work began on the site of the ship railway.

Bad weather would plague the construction almost as much as financial problems, as the Governor General would learn in 1894 in a brief from the company:

> Contracted for in June 1886, the completion of the railway in July 1889 — say in two half and two whole seasons — was impossible, even if all the conditions had been favorable, as half seasons are almost valueless for having work done ... The sub-contractors could only survey and measure the work during a few months of the year, and in consequence of this the whole of 1887 was lost, and part of 1888. A third season was nearly lost by the difficulties in obtaining labor and on account of heavy rains which kept the marshes flooded so long that it was impossible to begin the cuttings and embankments; and thus the work could not be properly started until 1889.

Work on the two dock sites and the right-of-way began in the summer of 1887, even though the financing had yet to be arranged in the aftermath of Cutbill & Lungo's withdrawal. Construction would not begin in earnest until the fall of 1888, when a veritable boom hit Amherst, and more than 400 people found work on the line, most of them laborers brought in from Quebec, many of them Italian immigrants.

Much of the work was done by shovels and picks, horses and dump carts. Large steam shovels were used in places. As work progressed, many of the local residents began to live in fear of the newcomers. Rum shops flourished in proportion to the labor camps, and many of the locals stayed indoors on a Saturday night when these rough-and-ready men, many speaking in a strange language, came into town to let off steam.

Most of these men were working for the Ontario firm of Dawson, Symmes & Ussher, which had the contracts to supply the ballast for the railbed, the dredging of both harbors, construction of the Tidnish breakwater, plate laying and masonry. Other firms were also involved: Rhodes and Curry of Amherst supplied the ties and built the machinery buildings, Harris & Co. of Saint John supplied the wheels for the cradle, and the Canadian Locomotive Co. of Kingston, Ont. was to supply the specially-built locomotives.

Ketchum's plans clearly show he intended a 2-8-0 "Consolidation" steam locomotive to be at the head of his amazing train. Coincidentally, these engines, the most powerful in their day, had been designed by Nova Scotia-born engineer Alexander Mitchell for a Pennsylvania anthracite railroad in 1866.

Officially, the engineering firm overseeing the project was that of Sir John Fowler and Sir Benjamin Baker. Ketchum was resident head engineer, and Fletcher T.S. Kelsey, who had worked in England on the second Tay bridge became the supervising engineer. There was much fanfare at home and abroad, especially in America, where interest was high in light of Eads' failed attempt to build the Tehuantepec railway.

As for Eads, he took no part in the Canadian project. The congressional wrangling and personal worries involved in his ship railway were reported have to so drained the once robust man, that he was ordered by his doctors to get some rest. He went to Nassau in the Bahamas, where he died March 7 1887.

Other Americans were interested because Yankees who

supported free trade between Canada and the U.S., men like Massachusetts Senator George Frisbie Hoar, proclaimed the undertaking to be the harbinger of a boom in international prosperity. Hoar, one of the founders of the U.S. Republican party, singled out the Chignecto scheme in this regard, in at least one speech in the U.S. Senate. *The Scientific American* endorsed the project, as did a host of other publications, some expert, some simply impressed by the grandeur of the scheme and the weight of the reputations of the men who were behind Ketchum, who published a barrage of pamphlets promoting Chignecto.

At the Fundy, or western terminal, crews gouged a huge hole into the mud of the LaPlanche River estuary. At Tidnish on the eastern terminal, a coffer dam was built to enclose an area 530 feet long and 300 feet wide. The water was pumped out and construction of the dock began, protected by two breakwaters forming a large semi-circle open to the Northumberland Strait.

The works were so large that even after more than a century of relentless erosion by the tides, both ends are visible from the air, and identifiable on a standard ordinance survey map. Tourists at the trailer park at Tidnish Bridge are often told the splendid masonry of the culvert over the Tidnish River was imported stone-by-stone from Scotland. In fact the stone masons came from Scotland, but the bridge, one of the most easily identifiable relics of the project, is made of sandstone from Northport, further along the coast, the same stone used in the construction of the Nova Scotia legislature building, some of the parliamentary buildings in Ottawa and many of the fine buildings of Boston and Philadelphia. The stone for the Fort Lawrence Dock came from nearby Wood Point.

All of this industry was directed from the company's Amherst office, a place known locally as Ballyhooly House in honor of the many lavish parties thrown to impress potential investors, curious and politically valuable politicians, and wring better deals out of suppliers.

Life on the job site was typically tough for the navvies. Even though Amherst was at most a scant 15 miles away, for most of the laborers through the week, it might as well have been 100 miles away. While the company's executives lived high on the hog at Ballyhooly House, or in their comfortable homes in Amherst and Sackville, N.B., the navvies worked, ate and slept amid the stone, sleepers and steel. As an indication of what their life was like, local legend tells the story of a navvy who decided to compliment the francophone cook on the unexpected luxury of finding raisins in the dumplings at the evening meal.

"Raisins?" said the cook. "Dem was not raisins!"

"Then what the hell was I eatin'?" the navvy demanded to know.

"Dem was pollywogs," the cook laughed. It was his style of cuisine to use water directly from the nearby bogs and brooks and add whatever happened to be in his bucket at the time to the menu.

On April 18 1888, Parliament was once again asked to give its blessing to a change in the contract, this time extending the completion date by one year. This was a direct result of the lack of response from investors. Further conditions were imposed on the company's performance. Specifically, the company agreed to pay a penalty of $1,000 per month for an additional two years to cover any delay after the new deadline had passed. There was some opposition, but Tupper assured Parliament the government was not being asked to pay money, "but simply enable English capitalists to furnish all the money required."

In spite of the initially lukewarm reception, the English investors eventually began to queue at the door of John G. Meiggs & Son. Meiggs' contribution was to be so important to Ketchum that one of the locomotives was to have been named after him.

In May of 1888, as Ottawa approved the CMTR's final engineering plans, Parliament passed the new Railway Act. This massive piece of legislation was intended to clean up the scandalous larceny being perpetrated by railway companies on the public purse. In many ways the conditions gradually attached to the CMTR's amended contract were far more binding than other railways had been obliged to accept. But within the new act was a clause which specified no bonds or debentures would be issued until one fifth of the cost of any railway project had been spent by the private sector. The intention was to force railway contractors to demonstrate some determination to actually see the work through, and commit their own funds before picking the government's pocket. So strict were the conditions laid out in the CMTR's contract, that Ketchum and his executives believed they were not affected by the new rules. In any event, by that same month many of the original promoters, including Townshend and Clark, were replaced by a board of directors and the railway became, as C.R. MacKay noted, essentially an English venture.

The spurt of activity on the site that year was to be short-lived. Weather again slowed the work, then an economic squall broke when the British money markets, influenced as most are by the vagaries of the day, experienced a minor scare, forcing Meiggs to cable a warning that shares could not be issued until January. Only a meager supply of money was then available.

By March of 1889 it seemed these problems had been overcome, as contractors took $100,000 of common stock and a further $300,000 in preferred shares was sold. But now the impact of that overlooked clause in the Railway Act of 1888 made itself felt, for it prevented the company from marketing the last $700,000 of first mortgage bonds; these would not appear on the market until November of 1889.

This is the point at which it might be possible to lay the blame for the failure of the enterprise upon the government of the day. It appears that the company had anticipated, and was preparing to meet, any obstacle posed by the act when on Aug. 21 1889, W.M. Fullerton, one of the company's Cumberland County agents, sent a telegram to the government specifically asking if Sect. 299 of the act would have any effect upon the Chignecto construction. He needed an immediate reply to forward to Henry Kendrick, the secretary of the investors' group in London. That same day, Collingwood Schreiber replied by telegram: "So far as I read the section and subsection, it does not apply until the commencement of the operation of the ship railway."

Clearly the company's board was given a false sense of security by the government, whether by design or oversight; any plans the investors might have had to raise additional funds were set aside because of the confidence they had in Shreiber's response.

The Railway Act severely cramped the flow of money to the region, but it was the following year which would prove to be the watershed for the railway. By Aug. 11 1890, the *Halifax Chronicle* reported that more than 1,200 men were at work across the entire line: "Every man is engaged in it, from the directors, chief engineers, and the contractors to the day laborers has a personal pride in the undertaking."

But 1889 had closed with Ketchum writing to Meiggs to inform him that, with all the bad weather and lack of money, the work which was to have been completed within 16 months would now take until the summer of 1891. Prime Minister Macdonald was given the same news, along with the request that the penalty clause be struck from the CMTR's contract: "On the grounds that it had been self-imposed by the company simply to speed up financial bargaining then in progress."

Once again political allies came to the firm's rescue, this time in the form of Finance Minister George Foster, who by happy chance was also the MP for Saint John. It was Foster who replied on May 20 1890 that the government would indeed forego the penalty money, and given this breathing room, activity at both ends of the line resumed that summer. Then, once again, time and circumstance conspired against him and one could forgive Ketchum if he ever harbored the notion that God himself was determined to thwart the project.

The new obstacle arose in Argentina, where the British

banking firm of Baring Brothers had, as it turned out recklessly, invested in a bond issue that was to collapse as a coup brought about a sudden change in the political climate of the country. Barings was no ordinary lender. It had literally helped bankroll the growth of the British Empire over the course of its history, earning one family member a noble title and the position of viceroy in Egypt.

In the preceding years Argentina had been experiencing rapid economic expansion, spurred by the construction of an extensive railway network, for which Baring Brothers were supplying the capital. The loan default ordered by the new government caused an international crisis, soothed only when the bank's obligations were guaranteed by the Bank of England, which allowed the company and individual members of the family to pay the entire debt forced upon them.

That so well-founded a firm could suddenly find itself quite literally facing bankruptcy overnight sent a shock wave through the financial world, enough to make British capitalists in particular shy away from foreign railway ventures. Among the casualties in the collateral damage would be the firm of John G. Meiggs & Son, which had invested heavily with Barings. The immediate impact on the Chignecto railway was that there was no one to issue what was left (about half) of the $700,000 in mortgage bonds, and once again with money in tight supply, work at the site resumed after the winter of 1890-91 on a much smaller scale.

Conditions did not improve in the spring of 1991. As MacKay notes in his history:

> When Ketchum objected that the latest shipments of ballast material were substandard and unacceptable, the subcontractors replied that since "rumors are current with the public that Messrs. Meiggs and Son and those connected with the undertaking are in financial trouble," some work had to be done, however poor the materials immediately available, since cessation of work might aggravate Meiggs' worsening

position in England.

In spite of an uncharacteristic lack of opposition to the government's extension of the completion date to July 1 1893, the Chignecto scheme was now beginning to unravel. "That summer, as funds ran out," MacKay says, "construction at Chignecto came to a halt. At the time, some $3,500,000 had been spent on the site, the docks were nearly complete, one line of track had been laid, and the first of specially-designed locomotive engines ... was about to be shipped from Kingston. But funds were gone, and the chief subcontractors, the firm of Dawson, Symmes & Ussher, which throughout the spring had accepted half its fees in the form of promissory notes, now possibly worthless, quarreled with Ketchum and threatened to remove its plant from the site. Ketchum himself repeated rumors that high-handed financial intrigue had blocked sale of the remaining debentures at a reduced price, and at least one Maritime newspaper raised the specter of financial scandal. Still, few really regarded the stoppage as more than temporary, since less than $1,500,000 was needed to complete the line. *The Monetary Times* observed simply that the enterprise "has received an obstacle," and Meiggs informed Ketchum that negotiations for the sale of the remaining bonds, albeit at a discount, were again underway. The engineer was confident the work would be completed by the following summer."

By that fall, with nothing resolved and no solution readily in sight, it appears Ketchum's confidence was waning. His correspondence from this point on indicates he was undergoing a noticeable change in attitude, swinging from the hubris of only months before, to a state of near-desperation, and finally desolation.

This too has added to the folklore of the railway, for it has always been said that Ketchum died of a broken heart. Many of the popular histories written about him invariably include a verse he is said to have penned in a letter to Baker, as though it could be his epitaph:

71

There is a time, we know not when,
A point we know not where,
That marks the destiny of men,
To Glory or Despair.

Certainly Ketchum was becoming disillusioned, and frustrated, as he wrote Feb. 2 1893: "This undertaking is as sound as ever and better, but the difficulty is to make people believe it."

To Sir Leonard Tilley, Sept. 15 1894, he wrote:

I do not wish to speak of myself, but I cannot help saying it is dreadfully disappointing to find one's honest endeavors to benefit his country so little appreciated. I have done all I can to remove ignorance and prejudice but I am afraid it is a hopeless task.

Seven

One of the Most Astounding Frauds

Perhaps in desperation, Ketchum wrote to Sir John A. Macdonald in the autumn of 1890 suggesting the government had to "come to our aid in some way or another," and toying with the idea of getting a one million dollar loan.

He must have known the loan was politically impossible, and as MacKay notes, the economic situation was becoming equally impossible: "As Winter deepened, an atmosphere of failure began to settle about the project. Most of the engineering staff had left, and local people were making off with rocks and cement from the works. Perhaps of greater import was the rumor that the 100 pound bonds, which had once sold on the London market at a small premium, had sunk to 50 pounds in value."

In all this time Ketchum's constant lobby was becoming something of an embarrassment to the company, and Meiggs was finally forced to suspend him. But Ketchum would not be easily separated from his project: "He laid his initial hopes," says MacKay, "in stimulating a rousing approach by the press on both sides of politics," and arranged for MacKenzie Bowell, the Minister of Customs, to inspect the site. Although Bowell professed admiration for the work done, he hesitated to proffer financial help. Foster, too, promised only that if the application for assistance were put into a shape defensible in Parliament, the government would give it a favorable hearing. "As the ministers have not repelled us at the outset," Ketchum wrote, "I have now every hope of succeeding with patience and persistence."

This may have been a grasping at straws on Ketchum's part, but in any case, the matter was out of his hands, for it was the company which eventually broached the idea of an exchange of the unsold 350,000 pounds in mortgage bonds for 300,000 pounds in Canadian government bonds at three per cent interest. In addition, the company pledged to complete the line by July 1 1893. But even this may have sounded too much like a boondoggle for Finance Minister Foster, for although the Dominion treasury theoretically stood to make money on the transaction, it also put the government in the position of being a capital investor in the project, something Sir John A., Tupper, Pope and Foster himself had promised the House of Commons would not happen.

It was left to Foster to inform the company, on Jan. 5 1892 that: "the government was obliged reluctantly to come to the conclusion that under all the circumstances of the case it was not possible for it to promise to undertake any further formal obligations in relation thereto outside of those provided for in existing Statutes" and warned that, "the Company knows that from the inception of this scheme it was clearly and repeatedly stated in Parliament that the country was not pledged and would not be pledged to the undertaking beyond the payment of a fixed subsidy for a term of years after the works had been completed and then only on condition that they were kept in operation."

Clearly, at this point, the federal government had decided to cut the ship railway loose, but Ketchum was unwilling to give up, and asked Foster if it was possible for an order-in-council to authorize payment of the subsidy by July 1 1892 if all the capital was secured by that date. The request was firmly rebuffed, possible because officially

Ketchum was not a representative of the company, merely a suspended employee and shareholder, his role at this point being little more than caretaker of the deserted site.

Despite Foster's professions of support for the railway, Ketchum would come to mistrust the Saint John MP's intentions to the point where he would become almost paranoid about him.

On Sept. 15 1894, Ketchum wrote to Sir Leonard Tilley: "I would ask you to do me the favor to speak to Mr. W.H. Thorne in order that the *Daily Sun* may continue to write articles favoring the extension. For some reason or other the *Sun* has been ordered not to agitate further for the benefit of the Co. I fancy — but this is merely surmise — that Mr. Foster is not favorable and perhaps he instigated the stoppage of the agitation by the *Sun*. I can hardly believe it but if I am correct, it looks as if the government meant to repudiate the ship railway obligation altogether."

Even at this point Ketchum's political friends had not abandoned him. In May A.R. Dickey, the newest MP for Cumberland County told Ketchum the government would extend the completion deadline to July 6 1894, thereby keeping the project eligible for the subsidy. Once again there were conditions attached to this accommodation, the extension depended upon the work resuming and the remainder of the capital being secured.

Prior to this, however, the English shareholders had set in motion a chain of events that would shape the last chapter of the Chignecto ship railway's history. On April 4 1892, at the second meeting in a month, the shareholders had voted not to abandon the project, and had appointed Andrew Dryburgh Provand, the Liberal MP for the Blackfriars and Hutchesontown district of Glasgow, to go to Canada and make sure the work resumed.

Here again circumstances were to conspire against the project, for it was in the spring of that year that a series of railway scandals broke in Ottawa which made potential British investors all the more wary of Canadian railway schemes. The British shareholders moved to make up for this setback by going directly to Sir Charles Tupper, who was then staying at Canada House in London, telling him that three quarters of the work had been completed before it ground to a halt in 1891, and seeking more financial aid and extension of the deadline to July 1 1895.

Tupper offered little help saying only that once the remaining private funding had been secured, the deadline would be extended. This merely reinforced the Catch-22 situation faced by the company. It felt it could not secure more investment without a further show of faith from the Canadian government, which was for its part requiring the company to first raise the private capital. If Macdonald had been a whole-hearted supporter of the Ship Railway, his successors certainly were not. Macdonald died in 1892, and was succeeded in rapid order by Senator J.J.C. Abbott and then John Sparrow Thompson.

In spite of his being a native Nova Scotian (and perhaps because, as some claim, he was a Halifax man beholden to the Halifax merchants) Thompson was less supportive of the railway than Macdonald. But then again, Thompson's tenure was beset by national crises which demanded more of his attention.

In April of 1893 Provand cornered Thompson and Charles Hibbert Tupper (son of Sir Charles), in Paris at the International Tribunal on the Bering Sea, determined in his Manchester-born way to get a commitment from the Canadians. But Thompson, who was focusing his efforts on the greater issue of national sovereignty, simply told Provand that Paris was neither the time, nor place, for an argument, and instructed him to send all the documentation to Ottawa for his bureaucrats to study.

Provand crossed the Atlantic in October of that year: "The results of this second trip contrasted unfavorably with those of the first," says MacKay. "The new subcontractor, James Ross, had refused to accept payment in company bonds, and work remained stalled." In Ottawa, Provand's abrasive bargaining stance hurt his position. Upon learning that the government had reiterated by order-in-council its refusal to give financial aid, he repeated the request for a time extension and threatened that "it will certainly create a very bad impression in financial circles" if the extension were refused, since, "Sir Charles Tupper's last words to the Deputation were considered as distinct promise of necessary extension of them." Thompson replied tersely that the "subject will be considered by Council as one on which the Government is perfectly free to grant or refuse", and that "your attempt to fasten a promise on us will not do." This marked a decided souring of the relationship between Provand and Thompson, obliging the Scot to embark for home in January of 1894 with a second refusal of financial assistance.

By June of that year Ketchum's hopes were buoyed yet again when the English firm of Pearson & Son of London signed a contract picking up where the unfortunate Meiggs had been forced to leave off. Redoubling their commitment, the original shareholders purchased the remaining bonds, in effect raising all the capital that was estimated necessary to finish the job. In triumph, no doubt, Provand cabled Thompson on June 28: "We have now secured the Capital to complete the Chignecto Railway and have settled with first class firm of contractors to commence the works immediately we secure an extension of time sufficient to complete them in two years for which I now apply on behalf of the Company."

Provand was acting on the assurances of Sir Charles Tupper that the Catch-22 created by the 1889 order-in-council had indeed been resolved. Now embroiled in a political battle over the Manitoba school question, Thompson burst the bubble, saying the matter could not be given immediate attention. It is this apparent intransigence that supports the notion that Halifax merchants were working behind the scenes to destroy any chance of the ship railway succeeding, and in so doing to blunt Saint John's competitive edge.

Provand took his case directly to the Governor General, Lord Aberdeen, pointing out on Aug. 3 that 3.5 million pounds had been spent on the project, and raising the possibility of expanded business: "It is their (the investors') intention to construct increased wharfage, coal tips, lumber and coal depots, plant for creosoting railway ties, etc. They are also prepared to create traffic from the commencement by the promotion of steamboat companies or subsidizing existing lines by free transport or otherwise. To carry out these intentions will take a very large sum in excess of what will be required to complete the original works and the whole of this outlay will be made in Canada."

In many respects the memorial presented to Lord Aberdeen is pitiable reading, for Provand lays out in detail all the adversity facing the project since its inception, at various points laying blame for delays on weather, labor shortages, international monetary scares and geography. At this point too, it appears supporters of the scheme had become sufficiently desperate to equate the failure to finish the project with a smear on the good name of the Dominion.

This prospect was raised by members of the company and members of the House of Commons. In a letter to Sir Leonard Tilley, in September of 1894, Ketchum wrote:

> I have just rec'd a letter from an able financier in London who gives his opinion as follows: "I cannot think however that upon final consideration the counsel can honorably refuse a further extension of time, and should they nevertheless do it cannot resound to their credit in any manner whatever and would undoubtedly cause a sensation here amongst the present financial friends of the Dominion." I have heard similar expressions from other well known stockbrokers in London.

Ketchum did not bother to name his sources, and it is unlikely Sir Leonard bothered to inquire, for the argument was already quickly gaining weight. Tupper had already raised the dreaded prospect in the House, and in his undated memo, Dickey warned: "I submit that the overpowering consideration in the present position of affairs is the credit and good name of Canada with the financial public. The most prejudiced person will admit that it is not sufficient that Canada should show that there is no LEGAL claim upon her for this subsidy. It will be generally concluded that in order to escape reproach, Canada must show that no MORAL claim exists. This country is and must necessarily long be a borrower in the London markets and her credit is of the very greatest importance to her. From the necessities of the case railway extension on any large scale in Canada can only be effected by subsidies granted in aid of roads and these subsidies must necessarily be given without a time limit. The action of the government in this instance will therefore most materially affect the prospects of any railway enterprise in Canada."

To hear Dickey, Foster and Tupper tell it, the fate of all future railways in the country hung upon the success or failure of the Chignecto ship railway. "It must be remembered," said Dickey, "that unless the case of Canada is morally an impregnable position those who might lose money by the refusal to extend the time in this case would be left with a bitter sense of wrong treatment and would probably be able to impress their views on their friends and associates in the financial world in London, whose sympathies would naturally go to them and would have little opportunity of hearing the Canadian side of the case."

Of course this tactic was just so much smoke and mirrors, for as time would prove, other Canadian railway ventures did survive the Chignecto failure, and as C.R. MacKay notes, the project was receiving very little press attention in the London financial periodicals by this time — an indication that British interest in the scheme had already evaporated.

All of the pleading was to no avail. By September the political climate in the country was such that Thompson, on the advice of John Haggart, the new minister of canals and railways, did not dare raise the possibility of yet another extension of the deadline. Still, C.R. MacKay says, government support for the railway had not expired. In

October of 1894, the shareholders sent another deputation to meet George Foster in London, with Tupper again present. According to Tupper, Foster assured them: "that the government will take this matter up as was promised ... and we will give it our best consideration on the grounds of what might be called moral obligations."

According to MacKay the fact Foster made this statement after Haggart had reported negatively on the idea of pressing the matter in Parliament implied the project had not been abandoned. This ignores the possibility that Foster was simply saying what the English shareholders — to whom he owed no political debt — wanted to hear simply to be rid of them, for by May of 1895, from the safety of Canada, Foster was reporting that it would be impossible to consider any monetary bills and promising the matter would be reviewed "next year."

As 1896 opened, Charles Tupper was back in Ottawa serving as Secretary of State in a government led by MacKenzie Bowell, after John Thompson had died so suddenly at Windsor Castle. It was only a few months before Tupper was to become prime minister for his ill-fated 96-day tenure. At this point, MacKay contends, "with Sir Charles Tupper, the railway's leading political supporter, now in a position to offer more than verbal encouragement, the CMTR appeared destined to acquire a new lease on life. The long-awaited order-in-council passed quickly, recommending that legislation be introduced during the current session to extend the completion date. However, before the government could introduce a bill to renew the subsidy agreement which had lapsed in July 1894, a private member's bill was needed to renew the charter of the company."

Here again Ketchum's hopes would be dashed, for after a bitter debate in which the project was condemned as a "bolstered scheme," and a swindle, the bill was defeated by a vote of 55-54. Still, Ketchum's political allies stayed with him. Two weeks after its defeat C.V. MacInerney, the New Brunswick Tory who had sponsored the bill, moved to have it restored to the order paper, stating the renewal of the charter did not automatically ensured renewal of the subsidy. In spite of more vehement protests, like that of Ontario Liberal J.F. Lister who called it "one of the most astounding frauds of the present century," the house voted 80-63 to restore the bill for another debate. Analysts like MacKay say the debate "convincingly documents Haggart's and Thompson's 1894 reading of the parliamentary mood, a political reality which Tupper, in London, had been able to ignore. Moreover, in the spring of 1896, as the government struggled mightily to obtain passage of the Remedial Act before the 25 April dissolution of Parliament, no further debate could be devoted to this local project of a railway across an isthmus. Tupper did make one last effort on behalf of the company. A 22 May order-in-council promised to deal with the matter during the next session. This declaration was almost completely meaningless, since clearly no action could be taken unless the Conservatives were returned with an increased majority, the least likely outcome of the impending election. Tupper's failure to obtain even the charter renewal, and the subsequent defeat of the Tories at the polls, marked the end of hopes for the completion of the railway."

Up to this point the Chignecto ship railway had survived three federal elections and five prime ministers: Macdonald, Abbott, Thompson, Bowell and Tupper. It would not survive Sir Wilfred Laurier's Liberals, but curiously enough, it would not disappear until the administration of Sir Robert Borden's Conservatives.

Eight

I Thought This Chignecto Business Was Dead

On Sept. 8 1896, Henry George Ketchum dropped dead of a heart attack outside the swank Amherst Hotel on Victoria Street. In the fashion typical of the times, his obituary in the proceedings of the Institution of Civil Engineers noted:

> Mr. Ketchum, who had been in indifferent health for some months, died suddenly ... His enthusiasm and confidence in the ultimate completion and success of this great undertaking never wavered. With persistent, earnest effort he devoted himself for fifteen years to the promotion of the enterprise with which his name is identified, and, although baffled when the work was within sight of completion, he never lost hope and was ready to stake all in support of his opinions. Some months before his death he had selected the spot on the site of the great work of his life, where he now rests.

Thus was born the most enduring of the tales about the ship railway: that its creator died of a broken heart frustrated to have come so far and overcome so many personal and political adversities only to see it all wither before his eyes.

As one stands in the graveyard of the little Anglican

church at Tidnish, a veritable stone's throw from the arrow-straight railbed Ketchum had planned, it is an easy tale to believe. But even in death Ketchum could not escape controversy, between those who believe he is buried at Tidnish, and those who cannot find a grave marker in the church yard. Historian David Stephens has the answer to the mystery:

> His remains were interned in Sackville cemetery while his widow survived him by many years. In his will, he had left money for the belfry and bell of the Church of the Good Shepherd in Tidnish. His widow had erected a stained glass window there in his memory.

In fact, Ketchum was originally buried at Tidnish, then reburied, on the wishes of his wife, in Sackville, N.B. closer to the home she made there after his death.

The dedication of the church window helps dispel the notion that Ketchum died both broken and broke. It is true he had more than just his professional integrity riding on the success of the Ship Railway, for as he told Sir Leonard Tilley after expressing fear the government was about to abandon the project: "If so it is a very great hardship to the investors and also to myself it means ruin for I have a large interest at stake both professionally and pecuniarily."

The fact that Sarah Milner Ketchum lived a well-to-do life long after his death, although partly depending on her own family's fortune, tells us that perhaps Ketchum, at that point was fretting about his imagined ruin more than he was experiencing real financial problems. The popular versions of ship railway history would have us believe the CMTR scheme died with Ketchum, but in reality Provand carried on his efforts to revive the company, albeit in name only, until he died sometime in 1914.

Realistically, however, the railway had died long before Ketchum, for no real work had taken place since 1891.

Just six days before Ketchum collapsed, Provand was in Ottawa, attempting to convince the new prime minister, Sir Wilfred Laurier — who had voted against renewal of the CMTR charter — to help finish the work. This proved to be a wasted effort. For too long the project had been known not just as a Tory scheme, but as one of the worst examples of their profligate squandering of Dominion resources. Laurier made no secret of his disdain for it: "The very name of Chignecto stinks in the nostrils of the Canadian people," he said. "The scheme has been denounced from the first as a job..."

Apparently the genius of the Chignecto ship railway did not fit Laurier's vision of the Canada to whom the twentieth century would belong, and he was not swayed by the assertions of ardent supporters like A.R. Dickey, that Canada's reputation would suffer internationally. By the end of the decade the plan was almost certainly beyond revival, and Provand's efforts switched from attempting to restore the scheme to mitigating the loss of the investors' money. If a eulogy was needed for the project, it was provided in a report to a privy council subcommittee Jan. 27 1898:

> Bearing in mind the almost universal testimony of experts and practical men of all shades of opinion that it is no longer possible to believe that this enterprise can become a commercial success under any circumstances (we) are of the opinion that the scheme cannot be regarded as one of such public utility as would warrant an application to be made to Parliament for a renewal of the lapsed subsidy.

Adding fuel once again to the fire of those who suspect a Halifax conspiracy against the railway was the membership on the committee of William Fielding, federal minister of finance.

Fielding, a former Halifax newspaper editor, had no doubt relied on Halifax merchants to finance and support his way into both the premiership of Nova Scotia, and the cabinet of Sir Wilfred Laurier, but no one as yet has produced evidence to show it was he who took up any Halifax cause to kill the Chignecto railway. There is no "smoking gun" as it were. To Fielding's credit, it appears he wasn't as willing to let the matter drop as quickly as some of his cabinet colleagues. According to MacKay's history: "Upon receipt of a letter from the trustees (March 1911) Laurier had turned it over to Fielding with the comment, "I thought that the Chignecto business was dead."

All that remained of the railway's history after Laurier's election victory is the story of protracted negotiations between the investors and the Canadian government in the hope of salvaging something from the project. In the end, the rails were taken up and relaid on the Intercolonial, the bricks and stone of the pumphouses torn down and used as fill at Tormentine, for which the investors were paid about $100,000 by the federal government.

It is a cruel irony, however, that the railway is remembered because it did not succeed. Often forgotten amid the political papers and economic navel gazing over the probability of success and failure was the spirit the enterprise stirred across Canada at the time: "Should the scheme prove as successful as anticipated," *The Dominion Illustrated* crowed in 1891, "it will be another triumph for Canadian genius and Canadian pluck, and add another to the list of magnificent public works whose construction has done so much to advance the commercial interests of the dominion. To have built the first successful ship railway in the world will be an honor not unworthily held by the young nation that already claims possession of the greatest of the world's great lines of railway transportation."

C.R. MacKay has a definite view that the railway failed because of an entrepreneurial failure (see the Appendix) but it would be a mistake to fix upon one single cause or event that might have occurred in such a politically and economically complex time.

It is worth noting that all the money that was to be raised from private investment had indeed been raised, albeit behind schedule, only to find new obstacles posed by political considerations. These took on some validity given the company's continued requests for more favorable terms. If there was one single cause leading to the failure of the project, it was more likely to be Schreiber's misreading of the Railway Act and the subsequent difficulties in raising the money rather than Liberal intransigence or a cabal of Halifax merchants, but the causes for investor wariness were many-fold, and beyond the control of the company.

First, Britain's own economy was working against the scheme. Investment money was becoming scarce at the very time the CMTR was trying to secure its last million dollars. Britain's mid-Victorian prosperity had peaked in 1873 when the economy collapsed. There was persistent pressure on profit margins that lasted until the mid 1890s and has been called a great depression. There was concern for markets and materials and the national rate of growth had slowed to below one per cent per annum — hardly an encouraging market for investors. Indeed, it could be said it was miraculous that the project found as much investor interest as it did, given the unorthodox nature of the proposal and the economy of the time.

At the same time, war had its detrimental affect on business. Mere uncertainty about the future shakes consumer confidence, throwing all investment into doubt as those with wealth convert it for security's sake into tangible assets like bullion. Any business investment represents a commitment to the future, and the greater the uncertainty, the more gunshy investors become. The era of the Ship Railway was definitely an uncertain time, with several major international events to shake the markets. Included among these were: the British bombardment and annexation of Egypt in 1882-83 to protect the Suez canal; the Anglo-French hostilities in the Sudan in 1898-99, which brought two armies to the brink of war at Fashoda; financial scandals surrounding the Panama canal including the bankruptcy of engineer Ferdinand Lesseps; the Spanish-American war, the Boer war, the Boxer rebellion. All could be said to have contributed to the world money market's jitters and fits.

The story surrounding the Chignecto ship railway is a fascinating study of the dynamics of men, money, ideas and twists of fate. More often than not, although historians find it convenient to apportion blame, it is time and circumstance which conspire to foil men's dreams.

The final irony of the Chignecto Ship Railway took place in Ketchum's lifetime, but probably went unnoticed at the time. In 1875, in order to legitimize his proposal to put fully-laden ships on rail, Ketchum wrote of the Dioclus, an ancient Corinthian ship railway, and the benefits that had accrued to the city of Corinth centuries before. The "railway" connected the Gulf of Corinth with the Gulf of Aegina, across a four-mile-wide land bridge. In March of 1882 — as Ketchum was trying to convince the Canadian government of the superiority of his technology — a canal was begun to cross this isthmus, four miles long, 100 feet wide and 26 feet deep. It was completed on Aug. 6 1893.

Picture Section

Map of the region from Ketchum's propsectus (Fort Beaausejour, NHS).

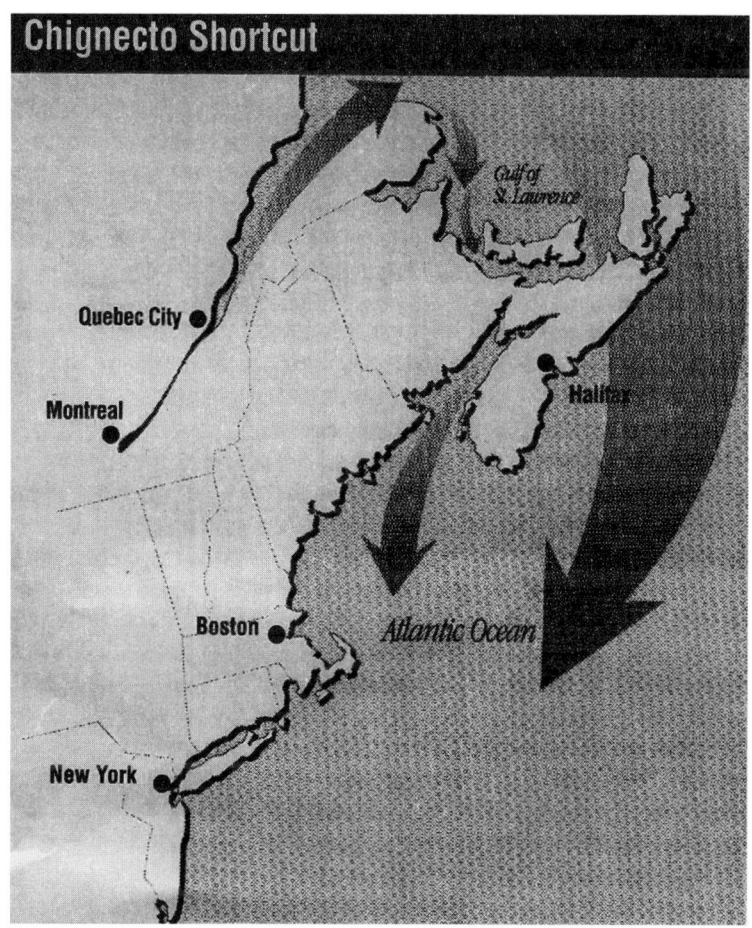

Frank Myrskog (Map of shortcut).

Left: Henry George Clopper Ketchum (Fort Beausejour NHS).

Below: Ketchum's Sussex Vale line today (Jay Undersood).

Sir Benjamin Baker (Institution of Civil Engineers).

James Brunlees (Institution of Civil Engineers).

Sir John Fowler (Institution of Civil Engineers).

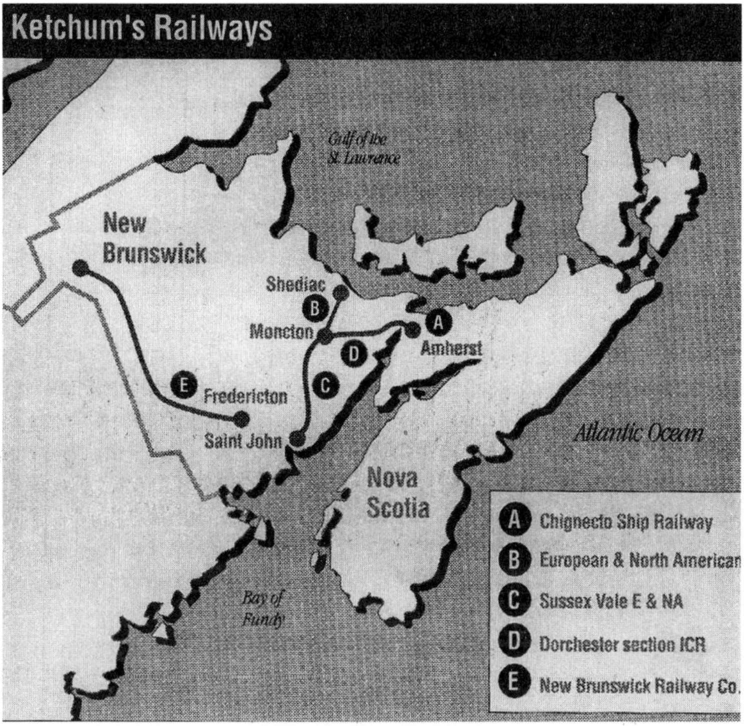

Ketchum's Railways

Map of Metchum's lines (Frank Myrskog).

The Saint John fire of 1877, a drawing by E.J. Russell (New Brunswick Museum).

The ill-fated Cunard ship **S.S. Oregon** (University of Liverpool).

Henry Ketchum as an older man shortly before his death.

*Left:
James Buchanan Eads
(Library of Congress)*

*Below:
Ketchum's grave in
Sackville, N.B. (Jay
Underwood).*

The fabled church at Tidnish, near the Tidnish dock (Jay Underwood).

Detail from Ketchum's original sketches (Tom McCoag, permission of Fort Beausejour NHS).

Ketchum's original sketch detailing the technology of the ship railway (Tom McCoag, permission of Fort Beausejour NHS).

An artist's concept, commissioned by Ketchum, of the ship railway in operation.

Samples of rail from the ship railway (left) and the Intercolonial Railway of the same period, illustrating the superior size of the CMTR track (Tom McCoag, permission of Fort Beausejour NHS).

Fort Lawrence Dock under construction, as printed in **Dominion Illustrated**, May 1896 (Public Archives of Nova Scotia).

*Tidnish culvert under construction (**Dominion Illustrated**, Public Archives of Nova Scotia).*

The culvert at Tidnish as it appears today (Jay Underwood).

*The CMTR's permanent way, near the crossing with the Intercolonial at Fort Lawrence (**Dominion Illustrated**, Public Archives of Nova Scotia).*

Appendix

KETCHUM'S FIRST LETTER TO THE TELEGRAPH

SIR, — The projected Canal from the Bay of Fundy to the Straits of Northumberland has occupied the attention of numerous commercial, political and scientific gentlemen for half a century. Surveys were made as long ago as 1823.

The illustrious Telford, founder of the Institution of Civil Engineers, reported on it in 1826. Later on, it was surveyed by Royal Engineers, at the joint expense of Canada, New Brunswick and Prince Edward Island. More recently, other eminent engineers made exhaustive surveys and reports; and, a few days ago, it was a topic for discussion in the Dominion Parliament.

Notwithstanding this, there has yet been no decided action taken towards the commencement of the undertaking, and its final achievement looms only in the distance. The assumed cost of such a work seems to be the principal reason why no steps have been taken to ensure its completion.

The time, therefore, seems opportune to discuss the feasibility of any project for the transportation of vessels which would answer all purposes at far less expense.

The undersigned is prepared to submit that a Ship

Railway would not only fulfill all the requirements, but, in many respects would be preferable to a canal, — that there is no engineering difficulty, either in the construction or in the operation of such a line; and that vessels, in full cargo, can be transported over the narrow neck of land which connects Nova Scotia with the continent, in perfect safety and at small expense.

It offers the following advantages over a canal: — Its utility would not be controlled or limited by the action of the tides or the direction of the wind. The transportation of vessels would, therefore, be more quickly performed. The maintenance, repairs and operating would be less expensive. The execution of the work would be more rapid, and the estimated cost can be determined more accurately. Lastly, its cost would not exceed one fourth of that of a ship canal.

There are so few natural obstacles in this place, that the Railway may be made, if necessary, perfectly straight and level from end to end. It would be important, however, to locate it on the firmest ground, and to avoid heavy embankments. To obtain this at the least expense, a few curves of large radii would be necessary; and the car or cradle which is to carry the vessel and cargo should be made with this view. The railway may consist of three parallel lines of track of the usual gauge. The width of the triple track would be about thirty-six feet. The rails should be of especial make and size. The tracks would be laid on longitudinal sleepers, secured to cross timbers extending the whole width. These would be bedded in ballast on the upland and rest on piles in the marshes. There would be about two miles of railway laid on piles; the total length of railway, eighteen miles.

The process of transportation would be as follows: — first, a platform car or cradle, made on purpose to receive the vessel and its contents, is placed on the railway. It rests on a large number of bogies, and is supplied with keel and side blocks. Its dimensions would correspond with those of the largest vessel to be transported. It is then moved from the railway to the stage of an hydraulic lift which is to be erected at each terminus of the line for the purpose of raising and lowering vessels by means of the hydraulic press. The stage, with the car upon it, is lowered to the bottom of the lift where it is ready to receive a vessel. The vessel is now brought from the basin, where it has been awaiting transportation, to the lift, and moored between the columns containing the hydraulic presses, exactly over the centre of the car. Pressure is now applied, and the lifting commences. The keel blocks are first brought to bear under the keel, the side blocks are hauled in, and the whole — vessel, car and all — are lifted clear of the water to the level of the railway. Couplings are now attached, and two or more locomotive engines haul them to the other terminus, where they are lowered to the sea by the same appliance. The time occupied in lifting a vessel would be about half an hour. The average cost would be about ten cents per ton for the whole transportation.

The cost of building a ship railway as described, and including hydraulic lifts and rolling stock, also with docks, or basins excavated to receive vessels at the lowest water, and ample margin for engineering and contingencies, would not exceed three million and a half dollars. I have the honor to be,

Sir, your obedient servant.
H.G.C. Ketchum,

Fredericton, April 5 1875

THE SECOND LETTER TO THE TELEGRAPH

Sir, — In my first letter addressed to you on this subject, many particulars were necessarily omitted, explanatory of the system proposed to be adopted, for raising the vessels to the level of the railway track; the method of transportation; and the construction of the railway and rolling stock.

It is now proposed to enter more largely into the outline of the scheme, sufficient to justify the assertion of the feasibility of a Ship Railway, and perhaps to satisfy the sceptical that it is quite within the bounds of practicability.

It will be necessary to submit, in the course of this and succeeding letters, the evidence upon which the conclusions have been based; and it will be shewn that the scheme is an adaptation of well-known principles and appliance actually in use — for other purposes, it is true but the practicability of which has been fully demonstrated and established beyond dispute.

It must be admitted, that if the transportation of vessels could be easily, safely and quickly performed by means of a Ship Railway, it would be desirable to adopt it in preference to a canal, on account of its immense saving of cost, its comparative speed of transportation, economy of maintenance, rapidity of execution; and freedom from the influence of tide, mud, wind or frost.

It is here again asserted, without fear of contradiction from any competent civil engineer, that a Railway can be constructed to answer all requirements; that appliances can be adopted to raise vessels steadily and easily, up from the sea level to that of a railway track; and that rolling stock can be designed and made to convey them from thence to any distance. Vessels can approach the terminus and be lifted on to the Railway at all times of tide, day or night. A half-tide canal can only be used six hours out of twelve.

Moreover, in the spring and fall, the season of navigation would be opened earlier and closed later than it could possibly be in a canal. There being no current in the latter, the ice would stay as in a pond, until melted away in the spring. And in the fall it would be frozen over before the navigation would close in the Gulf.

Thus for those precious few weeks at the close and beginning of the season, means would be furnished for the rapid transmission of goods, regardless of ice, wind or weather, whilst the canal would be useless. Let us, therefore, calmly and without prejudice discuss the feasibility of a Ship Railway, and judge whether we have or not sufficient data to pronounce upon its practicability.

The largest vessel likely to ply between Montreal and St. John, or from Quebec to Boston, would be a screw propeller of about 1,000 tons burthen, which would weigh with cargo and machinery about 2,000 tons.
The idea of raising a ship of this size out of the water might appear chimerical, were it not of a daily occurrence, both by means of marine railways and by the hydraulic lift.

Marine railways capable of carrying ships of 1,200 tons burthen, and machinery capable of hauling them out of the water, may be seen any day in Boston or Halifax.

The ship is first floated on to a cradle, which has been lowered into the water to receive it, and when it is secured in position by blocks, it is hauled up an incline by means of an endless chain and stationary engine. If there is any room for wonder in this operation, it is to wonder how such clumsy contrivances work at all, and then to wonder how they can be made to pay.

Nevertheless, here is an example of what may be done, although very inadequate for the purposes of a ship railway, such as is proposed for Baie Verte.

In hydraulic lift graving docks, the ship is raised vertically out of the water, having been first secured to a pontoon which sets on a stage acting between columns ranged on each side in which are placed the hydraulic rams. This pontoon is then raised, with the ship on it, and upon arriving above the surface of the water, the valves in the pontoon are opened and the water let out, so that it can be floated off the staging to any other place for repairs.

It is proposed to use this method of lifting at the terminus of the ship railway in preference to that of a stationary engine with an incline.

A few facts relating to the hydraulic lift erected in the Thames graving docks, London, will be interesting, as forming conclusive evidence of its practicability for the ship railway proposed.

The lift has been in operation upwards of ten years, and thousands of vessels have been raised and lowered upon it without the slightest accident. There are thirty-two columns ranged sixteen on each side, which contain hydraulic presses capable of lifting 200 tons each. The total lifting power is, therefore, 6,400 tons but deducting dead weight, the net available power is 5,780. The pumps are worked by a fifty horsepower engine, communicating with the presses by an aperture of 1 7/8 inch diameter. The raising and complete docking of a vessel occupies
about 25 minutes. The cost of the lift, with all machinery, was 25,000 pounds sterling; that of docking a vessel averages three pounds.

By dispensing with the pontoon, and substituting instead a cradle or carriage on wheels (which rests on rails laid on the stage, between the columns), there is an exact representation of what is proposed for each terminus of a ship railway, with one exception, that the lifting force will not require to be so great. It is said there would be a great strain on the vessel when deprived of the support of the water, and that in case of old vessels, they might fall to pieces. Your correspondent does not see the force of this objection.

It is not proposed to carry rotten or unseaworthy ships. There was no such result in the Thames Graving Docks, where old vessels are obviously those requiring most repairs. The vessel would be propped up at numerous points by keel, bilge and side blocks, adapted to the vessel's shape, immovable when once placed in position, and therefore, supported as well as in the water. Certainly no vessel would be subjected to the strain it is likely to encounter in a gale of wind at sea.

In the next letter, the construction of the ship railway itself, as well as the rolling stock, will be treated at length;

likewise further evidence in support of the scheme will be given.

I remain, Sir, your obedient servant,
H.G.C. Ketchum
Fredericton, April 14 1875

THE THIRD LETTER TO THE TELEGRAPH

Sir, — The fact that no Ship Railway, of the description here advocated, is in existence, should not operate as an argument against the feasibility of one in such a favorable place as that proposed, in lieu of the Baie Verte Canal.

The experience obtained in marine railways on a small scale, as before stated, will exemplify the practicability of one of greater proportions.

If it be possible to convey a ship fifty yards by such limited means, it is quite likely that with improved machinery and appliances, vessels may be transported a much greater distance. It is not proposed to lift ships out of the water by an endless chain and stationary engine, for, since the introduction of the hydraulic lift, such antiquated machinery is, for the most part, abandoned. Nor is it intended to use the same application of power, for one or more locomotive engines would be a vast improvement upon the stationary engine. No incline is required, for once lifted out of the sea to the level of the track, there is a straight and level path upon which the vessel may be conveyed.

To render the transportation of ships successful for a distance of eighteen miles, new and improved appliances of every sort may be brought into requisition, so as to make it easy of accomplishment. Nevertheless, so far as they go, these marine slips seem to illustrate the ordinary and successful operation of raising and lowering vessels on an incline plane; the construction of a cradle or carriage capable of holding vessels; the system of blocking, by which vessels may be securely sustained in position, without strain, whilst the carriage is in motion, and several other details connected with the operation.

The railway track itself must be capable of bearing with ease the weights that are to be conveyed over it. It must be absolutely free from danger of settlement or subsidence, or upheaval by the action of the frost. The materials must be comparatively indestructible. If necessary, the employment of wood may be dispensed with.

Above all, it is necessary to find a location favorable enough to ensure the fulfillment of these stipulations. On this point there need be no apprehension.

A steel rail, six inches deep, and weighing one hundred pounds to the yard, should be adopted. Six of these rails laid on longitudinal sleepers of pine with cross ties, would distribute the weight of the ship and carriage, and form a permanent road-bed. The railway would then comprise a triple track of 4 feet 8 inches gauge, making a total of twenty-five feet.

In order to prevent subsidence, all deep embankments must be avoided; and that small portion of the railway which would necessarily come on marsh ground should be laid on a foundation of wooden or iron screw piles. It may be here remarked that wooden piles will last forever in the salt mud of the alluvial formation of Westmorland. As an instance of its remarkable preservative qualities, it may be mentioned that the piles used by the French during their occupation of Fort Cumberland are now to be seen as sound and perfect as when first driven. This mud also is impervious to frost, and consequently there would be no danger of upheaval.

On the solid ground or upland, upon which at least nine-tenths of the length of a ship railway can be located, the sleepers may rest on a dwarf wall of dry rubble masonry, running longitudinally under each rail, and the interstices filled with ballast or stone.

It is believed such a plan as this would secure complete drainage, freedom from injury by frost, and absolute solidity to the railway track. There is no necessity for bridges of any kind on the entire route.

If any small embankments should be required they should be made up of rock taken from the excavations. The masonry dwarf walls would not be expensive, for the stone could all be obtained from the cuttings, and would not have to be quarried on purpose.

Owing to the shallowness of the water in Baie Verte, the railway will have to be carried out to deep water on a foundation of iron screw piles, filled in, perhaps, with rip rap, so as to make a solid embankment. Here wooden piles would not answer, owing to the ravages of the sea-worm (tereda navalis), which would, in time, destroy any wooden structure under water along the Gulf shore.

The hydraulic lift at Baie Verte might be utilized as Graving Dock, for the accommodation of all vessels in the Gulf of St. Lawrence, requiring repairs or painting. There need be no interference with the service of a ship railway on this account, and no alteration of the terminus or further expense beyond that involved in the construction of a few pontoons.

It is needless to remark that a graving dock in this place would be an immense boon to ship-owners, and benefit and build up the surrounding country. The shallow water would be a facility rather than a detriment to such utilization of the hydraulic lift. The largest vessels may be thus raised and floated on pontoons, drawing no more than four feet of water, towed to the shore or grounded in any part of the bay to undergo repairs of any kind.

Another suggestion is offered. Upon the completion of the ship railway, one of the railway tracks may be used for the traffic of an ordinary railway in connection with a single line from Baie Verte to Cape Tormentine. This desirable advantage may be obtained without interference with the transportation of ships to such a purpose in connection with the traffic to Prince Edward Island.

I remain, Sir, your obedient servant,
H.G.C. Ketchum
Fredericton, May 21st, 1875

THE FOURTH LETTER TO THE TELEGRAPH

Sir,— In further pursuit of the subject of a Ship Railway for the Isthmus of Chignecto, I may be permitted to reply to some criticisms of the press.

I have, as you are aware, courted publicity ever since the scheme was broached, six and a half years ago. My plans were hung on the walls of the News Room in Saint John for two years after they were exhibited in the Mechanics' Exhibition. Every opportunity has been given to the public and to engineers to find fault with it if they could. After all this publicity, the worst that has been said is that it is a "novelty" and "an experiment." I think it deserves no such appellation; But let me say that if nothing were to be attempted that had "never been done before," the world would be at a standstill; there would be an end to all progress. We should never have been civilized, but simply have remained in our original savage state.

In 1718, Count Emanuel Swedenborg, who was a military engineer, and also the founder of the sect of "Swedenborgians," constructed a road for carrying laden vessels from Stromstadt to Idefjal in Sweden. This road was twenty miles in length, and passed over a very mountainous country. Swedenborg was made a noble for this service by the King of Sweden. I cannot inform you how long this road was used, but history tells us that Charles XII used it in the war with Russia in 1718 to transport cannon to the siege of Frederikshall, and sloops of war, galleys and large boats were then carried over it by what is described as a "rolling machine."

To go back still further, a ship railway was built and worked over the Isthmus of Corinth twenty-three centuries ago. Recent excavations in Greece have discovered the remains of this ship railway. It was called "The Dioclus." It was established from the harbor of Schoenus to the eastern extremity of Port Lechaeum. This Dioclus was nothing if not a ship railway, — polished granite stones having been used in place of iron rails.

The Dioclus was worked probably for two centuries or

more, until the Emperor Nero commenced a canal, which was never finished. It was in existence in the time of Aristophanes, B.C. 427, and was worked up to the time of the Peloponnesian war.

The object of the Dioclus was to avoid the difficulty of weathering Cape Malea, and the short cut through the isthmus made Corinth the most opulent city of Europe, for it became the emporium of trade between Italy and Asia. In similar manner St. John may become the distributing point for Canada of the West India trade when the Chignecto Ship Railway is finished.

This work, whether as regards constructing or operating, is, with our modern appliances and inventions, mere play compared with the Herculean task of the Dioclus, without dynamite, steam power, iron rails, or hydraulic lifts.

This Railway will be simply a Marine Slip extended, with hydraulic lifts at either end. Marine slips are used in the naval arsenals of every country of the world. Ships are dragged out of the water up an incline, more or less steep, by ropes, sometimes chains, the power applied being a stationary steam engine. The difference between the ship railway and the marine slip is that the former is longer and the track will be level or nearly so, and consequently vessels will be more easily hauled along it than on a steep incline, and they will not be liable to the same strain as on a slip.

The hydraulic lift is certainly not an experiment. It has been used ever since the erection of the Brittania bridge over the Menai Straits. It is in use at Anderton, Cheshire, England, for transferring laden vessels from the Trent and Mersey Canal to the River Weaver. Vessels with cargos have been raised and lowered by this means a height of fifty feet for many years, without the slightest accident or delay.

The lifts proposed for the Chignecto Ship Railway will be similar to those of the Thames Graving Docks on the North Woolwich Railway, near London, where vessels have been raised out of the water, for repairing purposes, for upwards of twenty years.

Stationary engines will be used to draw vessels off the lift and to set them in motion for some distance beyond, when a powerful locomotive will be all that is necessary to move the load the remaining distance. There are locomotives on this continent capable of doing this service.

I assisted in the construction of a work of great magnitude in Brazil. I allude to the Inclines of the San Paulo Railway, where loaded trains are hauled up a mountain half a mile high on a grade of five hundred and forty feet to the mile. These Inclines cost a million dollars a mile, and they were five miles long. The stationary engines used there are capable of drawing 5,000 tons on a level road.

We will not have to deal with such great weights on the Chignecto Ship Railway. We do not propose to carry Cunard ships. The lake propellors, three masted schooners and fishing vessels will be about the average of laden vessels to be transported. We must, however, be prepared to convey ships of larger size that may be seeking cargo. In effect, we must do whatever the Baie Verte Canal was designed to do. And, if I mistake not, we shall do it more speedily, more cheaply and more efficiently.

I will refrain, however, from making comparison with the Canal; that scheme is dead and buried. Requiescat in pace. Let us erect on its grave a monument of engineering skill and commercial enterprise more worthy of the nineteenth century.

I have the honour to be, Sir,
Your obedient servant,
H.G.C. Ketchum, M. Inst. C.E.
Fredericton, Nov. 16th 1881

KETCHUM'S FIRST LETTER TO TUPPER

Sir, — I have the honour to submit for your consideration certain papers on the subject of a Ship Railway, for the transportation of laden vessels from the Bay of Fundy to the Gulf of St. Lawrence, whereby the long voyage round the coast of Nova Scotia may be avoided.

The great interest manifested in the formerly proposed Baie Verte Canal; the costly surveys and explorations extending over a period of half a century; the discussions of the subject in the several Local Legislatures and the Dominion Parliament; the exhaustive investigation of a Special Commission appointed to consider its commercial advantages; the disappointment in the Maritime Provinces occasioned by the adverse report of that commission (not unanimous, however) all testify to the great and manifest importance of a shorter route whereby vessels may be conveyed from water to water.

The principal objection, however, to a Ship Canal was its great cost, estimated by various engineers from eight to twelve million dollars. The commercial advantages of such communication were, to a certain extent, undoubted. Any plan to attain the same object equally feasible and costing less than one half the money should deserve the consideration of the Government and Parliament of Canada. A project, therefore, that would stimulate the coasting and fishing trade between the St. Lawrence and the Bay of Fundy, benefit established undertakings, create new enterprises, and increase shipbuilding; should command, and undoubtedly will receive the earnest attention of the Government, provided it can be proved practical and feasible, not only in execution and working, but also as regards ultimate cost and probable returns on the investment. With the firm conviction that it will fulfill these conditions, that it is destined to effect these objects, I venture to lay before you, officially, the scheme of a Marine Transport Railway, the same that was published in the *Daily Telegraph*, St. John, six years ago; the plans of which were exhibited in the Mechanics' and Manufacturer's

Exhibition in St. John in 1875, and afterwards in the News Room of that city until they were destroyed in the great fire of 1877. Since the preparation of these plans, which did not receive much favor at the time owing to the novelty of the project, I have been greatly encouraged and fortified by coinciding opinions of eminent engineers on the practicability of the proposed undertaking.

I am indebted to James Brunlees, Esq., Vice-President of the Institution of Civil Engineers, for a description of a Ship Railway across the Isthmus of Suez, proposed by him and the late Mr. E.B. Webb, C.E. to the late Emperor of the French in 1859, in place of the Suez Canal now in operation.

Their scheme was to transport ships of the largest tonnage then in existence by means of locomotives of special construction at a speed of twenty miles an hour. The ships were to rest on cradles supported by numerous wheels and springs, resting on a railway composed of five pairs of rails, and level throughout its entire length. They reported that "a ship would be able to make better use of her sails on a railway than on a canal;" that the system would offer all the facilities that are provided by graving docks. "The ships' hulls can be examined," they said "even whilst on their cradles, during the passage from one sea to the other; and if repairs are needed, can be taken on their cradles to a reparing yard." They estimated the Ship Railway to cost one-seventh that of Canal, and the toll for passing over proprtionately less. The passage of the Isthmus was to occupy only sixteen hours.

In 1872, Mr. Brunlees reported on the practicability of a Ship Railway across Central America for ships of 1200 tons burthen. His report and that of Mr. Edward Woods, Member of the Council of the Institution of Civil Engineers, on this subject will be found appended to this letter.

The late Mr. John Woodward of St. John, was the first to propose a Marine Railway across the Isthmus of Chignecto. His proposition was designed, however, only for small vessels — not larger than schooners — and there were to be Marine Slips at each end to haul up vessels out of the water to the level of the land.

But the most notable scheme of all, is that of Captain Eads, across the Isthmus of Tehuantepec, the surveys for which are now proceeding. His design is also to employ a Marine Slip, or incline, at each end of the railway.

The employment of the hydraulic lift — the invention of Mr. Edwin Clark, C.E. — as at first suggested by Mr. Brunlees for Suez — makes a Ship Railway more practicable of execution in the Bay of Fundy.

At this locality the tides rise to a height of fifty feet. A Marine Slip would necessitate a railway under water, at high tide, five thousand feet in length, at a gradient of 1 in 100.

The most desirable location for a Ship Railway is that beginning at a port or dock to be formed in La Planche River, thence passing close to Amherst, along the ridge parallel with the Tyndall Road, thence along the left bank of the Tidnish River, to another dock to be formed at deep water at or near its mouth. The total length would be about eighteen miles. There would be nearly level gradient from end to end of the line. The curves would be few, and those of very large radii.

The nature of the ground, therefore, presents no engineering difficulties. There are no rivers or streams of any importance to cross, and no obstacles whatever to the construction of a most solid roadway.

So far as can be estimated without precise and definite surveys, the cost of a Ship Railway, with Docks, Hydraulic Lifts, Rolling Stock, Cradles and Stationary Engines, combined with an ordinary Railway of the standard gauge, from Amherst to Cape Tormentine, would not exceed four million dollars.

While the probable traffic might not justify the expenditure of $12,000,000 for the construction of a Ship Canal, no reasonable objection could be raised from any quarter to the expenditure of the lesser sum required in an undertaking that would accomplish the same object.

I request, therefore, that this letter and the

accompanying papers on the subject, may be laid before His Excellency the Governor General; and I have to state that capitalists can be found to guarantee the practicability of the scheme, and undertake the execution of all works named, including the Prince Edward Island Railway, on the promise of a reasonable subsidy from the Government.

I have the honour to be, Sir,
Your obedient servant,
H.G.C. Ketchum, M. Inst. C.E.
Fredericton May 15 1881

THE SECOND LETTER TO TUPPER

Sir, — I have the honour to address you again on the subject of the Chignecto Ship Railway.

I informed you in my last letter of what, in my opinion, was the best location for this Railway. It was that from Amherst to Tidnish, beginning at a dock to be formed in the La Planche River, thence proceeding to another dock to be constructed at the mouth of the Tidnish River, where a jetty would have to be built into Baie Verte as far as the 16 feet low water line.

It is absolutely necessary that a railway, to be capable of carrying large vessels with cargo, should be entirely free from danger of settlement or subsidence. This desideratum is obtained by the lcoation recommended, as it would avoid marshy ground, bogs and streams, and pass over upland ground entirely and through cuttings. There will not require to be any large bridges at all and but few embankments on the whole route.

The entrance from the Bay of Fundy would be at the mouth of the La Planche, which is very accessible to vessels from seaward, and which would be well sheltered from the wind on their approach to the hydraulic lift at Amherst. The approach at Baie Verte would be nearly the same as that designed for the Ship Canal.

It will be seen at once, by reference to the map, that the undertaking of a Ship railway is not nearly so formidable as that of the Canal.

By enlarging and straightening the La Planche River to Amherst, the length of the railway may be reduced to sixteen miles.

There is, therefore, no other part of the Isthnmus of Chignecto which provides so short a transit, with ports so accessible and ground so solid.

The advantage to Amherst by improving the port, apart from the benefits to be conferred by the Ship Railway, would be very great.

The hydraulic lifts would be largely utilized for the purposes of repairing vessels at Amherst, when it is taken into consideration that about two million tons of shipping are annually cleared from the Bay of Fundy ports alone, and large numbers of vessels now seek repairs in the United States, which could be more easily and cheaply done at Amherst.

The same may be said of Tidnish, where all the vessels of the Gulf of St. Lawrence would seek such a handy refuge for repairs or cleaning and painting.

I now come to a more important matter, showing how the Ship Railway may be turned to profitable account in other ways besides those mentioned. It is that the Ship Railway, and the Railway to Cape Jourimain, and steam communication to Prince Edward Island should be combined in one scheme.

The line which has been surveyed from Amherst to Cape Jourimain, via Tidnish, passes so close to the line of the Ship Railway that one could not be built without interfering with the other. A part of the Ship Railway — say one of the three tracks — could be used without additional cost to the country; and, with occasional sidings or turnouts, it could be worked as an ordinary railway for the conveyance of passengers and freight. In winter time it could be used entirely for that purpose and as a double track railway.

I have thus endeavored to show that, even in case of failure of the Ship Railway to transport steamers and other vessels in cargo, all the work of which it is composed are capable of utilization. But, in stating this as one of other powerful arguments for its adoption, I do not mean to convey the idea that there is the slightest doubt in my mind, or in that of any civil engineer, of the entire feasibility of its accomplishment for the purposes for which the Ship Railway is proposed. On the contrary, the mass of engineering testimony already presented to you in my pamphlet is, I think, quite conclusive as to its practicability in every detail.

The cost of the Ship Railway, with all its appurtenances of docks, lifts, enlarging and deepening of harbors or approaches and jetties I estimated at four million dollars, with the Prince Edward Island Railway included.

I propose to raise this money by forming a Company, under Charter of a special Act of the Dominion Parliament. The Company will look to the Government for a guarantee of interest on the cost, or a subsidy for a term of twenty years. The Company will provide security for the due performance of the work, and to guarantee the safety of vessels transported. The Company will satisfy the Government by practical demonstration of the safe transport over one mile of ship railway of a steamer of 1,000 tons burthen, and by raising and lowering said steamer in the hydraulic lifts in full cargo, before recieving from the Government any instalment of subsidy.

The Baie Verte Canal was estimated to cost three times as much as the Ship Railway, and the interest on the cost of the Canal would equal as much as $600,000 for all time, to say nothing for its maintenance and repairs.

The Company will keep the railway in repair and work and maintain it, pay the cost of construction, and insure vessels using it, for certain tolls and fees to be hereafter established with the approval of Government, and also a Governnment subsidy of two hundred thousand dollars per annum limited to twenty years, by which time it may be expected the railway will pay for itself.

In requesting the favorable consideration of the Government to this proposal, I need scarcely enumerate the advantages to the Dominion, and especially to the Maritime Provinces, that may be acquired by the transportation of steamers, and sailing craft of all descriptions, without removal of cargo, across the Isthmus of Chignecto, and thus avoiding the tedious, dangerous and expensive voyage around Nova Scotia.

The mines of coal and iron, the quarries of freestone and plaster, on the Bay of Fundy would thus find new markets for their productions in Quebec and Ontario.

St. John might then become the emporium of the West Indies trade for the Dominion. Steamers laden with flour, pork and other western products could go all the way from Chicago to St. John without breaking bulk, and return thence to the west with products of the West Indies, and coal and stone.

A class of vessels that might come through the Canadian lakes and canals, but could not face the Atlantic coast of Nova Scotia, would be able to frequent Saint John and develop new trade. The products of the North Shore, in fish and lumber, would thus find an outlet in the Bay of Fundy and the United States. Prince Edward Island would be especially benefitted by the easy route afforded for all its products to the United States and elsewhere. It may be here remarked that the Straits of Canso are often blocked up with ice until late in the season, when there is free water communication elsewhere in the Gulf and River St. Lawrence. New fishery and other enterprises of all kinds would spring up. Vessels would be built and outfitted in the Bay ports of Nova Scotia and New Brunswick to carry on fisheries in the Gulf. American fishing vessels would also take advantage of the short cut to carry or send their cargoes of fish to Boston. All would be benefitted by the new development of trade that this Ship Railway would cause to be established.

Much, if not all, depends on the action the Government will take in this matter; or in other words, the aid which the Dominion would grant the undertaking. Under the conditions mentioned, all the risk would be taken by the Company. It could not, however, be expected to be remunerated without Government help. It would be some time before the expected trade would be developed, and the tolls would require to be put at a very low figure for its encouragement at first.

May I request, therefore, that this proposal may receive the favourable consideration of the Government, and will you favour me with an early reply? On receiving encouragment from you I am prepared to form the Company and make the necessary surveys and plans to lay before the Government.

I remain, Sir, your obedient servant,
H.G.C. Ketchum,
Fredericton, Nov. 7th, 1881

FROM C.R. MacKAY'S article — "Investors, government and the CMTR: A study of entrepreneurial failure," *Acedeinsis*, Vol. IX, No. 1, Autumn, 1979.

Years later, lingering doubts about the abandonment of the Chignecto railway coalesced into a romantic interpretation of its history. Even the 1931 Surveyor Commission, which concluded not only that a canal at Chignecto would fail to pay even its annual operating costs, but that such a facility would not improve local commerce, failed to dispel the "Maritime Rights" interpretation of the Ship Railway, the view that an economic venture beneficial to the Maritimes came to naught through lack of federal interest. Yet this view is almost completely wrong.

In the first place, the federal government demonstrated a great deal of interest in the railway, initially encouraging the venture and later acceding again and again to the company's request for changed contract terms. The latest completion date at which the company would remain eligible for an annual operating subsidy was extended from 1889, first to 1890 with a penalty clause, then without a penalty clause, then to 1893, and finally to 1894. The government attempted to extend the completion date still further, abandoning the measure only when the impossibility of passing such a proposal in the House of Commons became apparent. In each instance, the time extension was necessitated by the company's inability to raise private capital for the project, and only a federal government promise effectively to pay interest on the invested capital gave reason to hope that the capital might ever be raised. By the time the investors were ready to proceed, mounting political opposition to the railway prevented the government from making further alterations to the contract terms.

This growing political opposition, acknowledge by Ketchum in 1893, apparent to Thompson in 1894, and forcibly impressed upon Tupper two years later, deserves some consideration. Partly it was due to the public opprobrium into which the railway had fallen, and which

Laurier cited in 1898 as the ultimate obstacle to additional aid to the CMTR. Early plans for the railway had been greeted by widespread fears that a ship lifted from the water in this manner would simply fall apart, and while Ketchum produced arguments and authorities to prove otherwise, this scepticism provided the base for one sort of political opposition to the Ship Railway, partisan opportunism. One of the project's most virulent parlaimentary critics, J.F. Lister, was allenged to have admitted "laughingly ... that Chignecto had been a club with which to beat the government." As delay followed delay, spreading public confusion about the railway's financial position, this opportunism became a self-fulfilling prophecy. But a second level of political opposition also contributed to the demise of the CMTR. From the outset, the government had made clear to the company that it could not expect the operating subsidy before the work had been completed. Mackenzie and Blake warned that the promoters would eventually ignore this contract stipulation, which they did. Whereas the government might be willing to overlook a company's obligations in the interests of completing a work demonstrably of considerable importance, such as the Canadian Pacific Railway, the CMTR hardly deserved similar treatment.

In fact, throughout the period, no one had ever convincingly demonstrated that the Chignecto Ship Railway would be of much commercial significance. In 1875, the Young Commission had shown that the route could never be of national importance, and even Lawrence's minority report, which argued that the justification for the line would be the regional traffic its own construction might subsequently generate, was unable to identify the traffic. Throughout the 1880s, Ketchum's enthusiastic estimates of potential isthmus traffic were wildly improbable, except on the assumption that the railway would stimulate a shipping boom. For instance, his 1882 estimate that 600,000 registered tons of shipping would use the line annually (an estimate which Tupper cited in introducing the project to Parliament that spring) was equivalent to two-thirds of the total tonnage registered in the Maritimes that year. Ketchum's vague indications of where this traffic would come from, his expectation that traffic would be considerably lower during the first years of operation, his predictions of a vastly increased Maritime commerce in the 1890s, and the fact that the company had applied for a subsidy to run a line of steamships which was supposed to constitute a major part of the newly-generated traffic, convincingly demonstrate that even the project's chief promoter did not believe current shipping requirements justified a Chignecto Ship Railway. The Ship Railway, predicated not upon a stable economy but upon a boom of quite noble proportions, was an euphoric expression of Maritime economic attitudes in the 1880s, and the decine in Maritime shipping in the next decade merely emphasized a fact which had always been apparent to serious critics of the line. Mackenzie doubted its utility in 1882 and in 1896 Peter Mitchell concluded a debate on the railroad by declaring that "this is the first time that I ever saw an important measure of this kind, involving an expenditure of nearly $4,000,0008 pass through this House without anyone being able to show any practical benefits to result from it." By 1898, the gross error of early traffic estimates had become apparent to everyone in Parliament, and a decade later, even Provand conceded the point. Indeed, the popular notion that the Ship Railway was a victim of the decline of the Maritime economy at the end of the nineteenth century is but a more sophisticated version of the "federal-stab-in-the-back" outlook. The Chignecto Ship Railway failed for financial, political and finally economic reasons. While no one of these considerations would have been enough to defeat the project alone, together they made certain its collapse.

Epilogue

Contemporary interest in the challenge of crossing the Chignecto isthmus was revived in the late 1950s, when New Brunswick tycoon K.C. Irving began proposing construction of a canal.

Irving promised to set aside as large portion of his considerable real estate holdings around Saint John (where he owned the paper mill, an oil refinery and numerous other ventures) for the creation of an industrial complex expected to benefit from the same traffic envisioned by Henry Ketchum.

The idea was one of Irving's least successful. He gained the ambivalent support of New Brunswick Premier Louis Robichaud, but little else. In the meantime, the history of the ship railway was revitalized, notably in a series of magazine articles by Cumberland County historian Stanley Spicer.

To Spicer belongs the credit for the creation of what C.R. MacKay calls the "romantic" version of events surrounding the CMTR. But without Spicer's efforts, it is likely a lot less would be known about the Ship Railway. And, all these years after Ketchum's death, the challenge of Chignecto still taunts Maritimers, who continue to occasionally contemplate ways to circumvent the Atlantic

Ocean.

One of the more intriguing proposals is found in Jeffrey Holmes' novel "Farewell to Nova Scotia." In his lighthearted look at provincial separatism, Holmes' protagonists attempt to build a canal along the Missaguash River using a "nuclear knife." This series of small, controlled nuclear blasts is intended first to open a canal to harness Fundy tidal power. Instead, the province slides away from New Brunswick along a geological fault, separating Nova Scotia from Canada, and sending it further out to sea: "The narrow cut was clearly visible at this height and there was water in it all the way. Nova Scotia was an island. The old dream of a Chignecto canal had come true, although not quite as planned."

More recently, however, Nova Scotia has placed its hopes for a more secure transportation link to the remainder of Canada in the twinning of the TransCanada Highway. Just about a mile from where the waters of the Bay of Fundy still slowly grind away at the foundation of the Fort Lawrence dock, the newly-expanded, now four-lane, Highway 104 has eaten away at some of the last visible traces of Ketchum's dream.

Bibliography

Although no single book has hitherto been published on the history of the Chignecto Ship Railway, there have nevertheless been several articles and references to it in other books. Among those used for this book were:

BERTON, PIERRE — *The National Dream*, McLellan & Stewart, Toronto, 1970.

HANSARD (Reports of the debates of the House of Commons) May 9 & May 11 1882.

HIGGINS, BRUCE P. — "The Chignecto Ship Railway," The Engineer, *Journal of the Association of Professional Engineers of Nova Scotia*, November/December 1990.

HOLMES, JEFFREY — *Farewell to Nova Scotia*, Brunswick Press, Fredericton 1977

KETCHUM, H.G.C. — "The cost, feasibility and advantage of a ship railway across the Isthmus of Chignecto," *Chignecto Post* Publication, 1882.

"The Ismthian transit between the Bay of Fundy and the Gulf of St. Lawrence," Waterlow & Sons Ltd. London 1884.

The Chignecto Ship Railway, Damrell & Upham, Boston, 1893.

MacKAY, C.R. — "Investors, government and the CMTR: A study of entrepreneurial failure," *Acadiensis*, Vol. IX No.1 Autumn, 1979.

MIKA, NICK & HELMA — *Canada's Railways: A Pictorial History*, McGraw Hill Ryerson Ltd. 1978.

MILNER, W.C. — Unpublished papers, Saint John City Museum and elsewhere.

NEALE, JOSEPH P. — "The story of the Chignecto Ship Railway," *The Atlantic Advocate*, February 1979.

SPICER, STANLEY T. — "The Chignecto Ship Railway," *The Atlantic Advocate*, February 1960.

"The Chignecto Ship Railway," *Canadian Geographical Journal*, May 1961.

STEPHENS, DAVID E. — "The Chignecto Ship Railway," *Nova Scotia Historical Quarterly* (Journal of the Historical Society of Nova Scotia) Vol. 8, No. 2 1978.

Iron Roads: A History of Nova Scotia's Railways, Lancelot Press, Windsor, 1972.

WALLACE, F.W. — *Wooden Ships and Iron Men*, Mika Publishing, Belleville, 1976

Additional information on the railway can be obtained from the files of the Public Archives of Nova Scotia, the Public Archives of New Brunswick, Saint John (N.B.) City Museum, Mount Allison (N.B.) University Library, Fort Beausejour National Park, Aulac, N.B. The Cumberland County (N.S.) Museum, The Nova Scotia Museum (Halifax), and the University of New Brunswick (Fredericton, N.B.) Library.